MW00887511

VISIT:
WWW.PRISONPROFESSORS.COM/BOOKS

EARNING FREEDOM / PAPERBACK

9,500-day journey through federal prisons of every security level. From arrest, on August 11, 1987, through release, on August 12, 2013, we see a continuous focus on earning higher levels of liberty at the soonest possible time.

PRISON: MY 8,344TH DAY / WORKBOOK

Get guidandce on how to make progress through every day in prison. Learn the relationship between daily decisions and prospects for success. This book covers a typical day in a lengthy journey through prison, when every day counts toward preparation for success, with a 100 percent commitment.

SUCCESS AFTER PRISON / WORKBOOK

This self-directed workbook helps participants understand the relationship between adjustment decisions and prospects for success upon release. While crossing through 9,500 days in prison, the author leveraged a release plan to launch a life of meaning, relevance, and dignity.

PERSEVERANCE, 2023 / WORKBOOK

Daily lessons challenge participants to make intentional decisions. By documenting their pathway to success, participants can influence case managers, wardens, probation officers, and others who have discretion over their lives. Use this workbook to document preparations for success.

POST CONVICTION REMEDIES, 2023 / GUIDEBOOK

After a judge sentences a person to the custody of the attorney general, the person must learn how to self-advocate. Sometimes a person needs guidance and examples. This book will help.

WE PUBLISH
BOOKS/COURSES/VIDEOS
TO HELP PEOPLE IN PRISON HELP THEMSELVES

We Appreciate Sponsorship from Leaders
Who Support Scholarship Programs through our Nonprofit:

Prison Professors Charitable Corporation: EIN: 85-2603315

Emergency Disaster Services,
Lexington, Kentucky

Dr. Jeffery Gallups of the Ear, Nose, and Throat Institute
Atlanta, Georgia

Bill McGlashan,
Mill Valley, California

Mosssimo Giannulli
Beverly Hills, CA

Schmuel Jewish Foundation,
Los Angeles, California

Golden State Lumber,
Petaluma, California

Pandora Marketing,
Aliso Viejo, California

Earning Freedom
Dana Point, California

Etika, LLC
Irvine, California

FORWARD

My name is Michael Santos, and I am writing this personal letter to welcome every participant to this self-directed workbook on building a release plan. We hope that your institution offers our course:

» Preparing for Success after Prison

In the 30-hour, First-Step-Act-approved course, participants learn the value of self-directed efforts to improve:

» Communication skills,

» Critical thinking,

» Self-directed learning,

» Release Planning,

» Prioritizing,

» Creation of tools, tactics, and resources,

» Progress on the execution of the plan, and

» Documentation of progress.

Those tactics help to restore confidence and advance prospects for success. They worked for me. I am confident they will lead to a higher level of liberty for anyone who adheres to a values-based, goal-oriented adjustment.

Although I concluded my obligation to the Bureau of Prisons in 2013, I continue using this course's lessons. They are an integral part of the advocacy strategies our team believes will improve outcomes for all justice-impacted people. I also continue using plans to help me overcome the challenges I face.

Participants may find value in using these lessons to work through the crisis of a criminal prosecution and the collateral consequences that follow.

INCENTIVIZING A PURSUIT OF EXCELLENCE:

Our team at Prison Professors uses the courses we create to persuade stakeholders to support reforms that will empower the Bureau of Prisons to incentivize the pursuit of excellence. Those arguments led to Earned Time Credits in federal prison and Milestone Credits in state systems. We're continuing to advance those initiatives.

We must collect data to persuade stakeholders, including business owners, citizens, and administrators to join our coalition. Those influencers can show legislators why reforms that allow people to earn increasing levels of liberty through merit can improve the culture of confinement and contribute to community safety.

I began making those arguments more than 20 years ago while working through the depths of a 45-year sentence. I began serving that sentence during a different era. Legislators had passed laws that removed incentives, calling for truth-in-sentencing. If a judge imposed a lengthy sentence, lawmakers wanted people to serve the entire sentence.

Those legislative changes resulted in a larger prison population. As high recidivism rates show, they did not result in safer communities.

COALITIONS:

With our new course, we can present evidence that shows the positive results when people start sowing seeds early to prepare for success upon release. A researcher from UCLA is helping us collect data and publish findings in peer-reviewed journals. We hope those findings will lead to broader coalitions that will include:

» Prison administrators,

» Judges,

» Prosecutors,

» Probation officers, and

» Business leaders.

Together, we should work toward bringing changes in policies and laws that will empower administrators to incentivize the pursuit of excellence. Those incentives may include:

» Broader use of furloughs,

» Work release programs,

» Access to compassionate release and commutations.

We can only succeed in our work if imprisoned people invest in themselves. When people prepare for success upon release, we can show that we're working to make prisons safer and lowering recidivism rates.

To broaden the initiative, we've launched PrisonProfessorsTalent.com. This website is part of our nonprofit enterprise. It allows people with access to email, directly or indirectly, to document the systematic steps they're taking to build effective release plans. The website encourages people to memorialize their journey by:

» Engineering release plans,

» Showing the courses they complete, and

» Demonstrate the value they can add to prospective employers and stakeholders.

For more information, please send an email to our interns:

» Interns@PrisonProfessorsTalent.com.

Prison Professors Charitable Corporation
32565 Golden Lantern Street, B-1026
Dana Point, CA 92629

We hope all participants will become a part of the change we want to see in the world.

Respectfully,

Michael Santos,
Founder

PRISON PROFESSORS
Talent

Other Books by
Michael G. Santos / Prison Professors

Earning Freedom:
Conquering a 45-Year Prison Term
PrisonProfessors.com
(Shows strategies to build strength and discipline through long term)

Prison! My 8,344th Day: Workbook
PrisonProfessors.com
(Shows strategies to be productive through single day in prison)

Success After Prison: Workbook
PrisonProfessors.com
(Shows outcomes for people who use time in prison to prepare for success)

Perseverance Workbook
(Annual Edition)
PrisonProfessors.com
(Self-directed course to help people in jail or prison)

Release Plan Workbook
PrisonProfessors.com
(Self-directed course to help people in jail or prison)

Inside: Life Behind Bars in America
St. Martin's Press
(Insight to high-security prisons in America)

Preparing for Success after Prison—
FSA-Approved Course (SENTRY code PSAP)

ISBN: 9798854432146

Version: July 31, 2023

To Contact us, please visit:
www.PrisonProfessors.com
Books@PrisonProfessors.com

To receive our newsletter: Send invite to
Interns@PrisonProfessorsTalent.com
32565 Golden Lantern Street, B-1026
Dana Point, CA 92629

Contents

INTRODUCTION TO RELEASE PLANS

While lying inside a solitary prison cell, I needed hope. Biblical passages frequently inspired me, especially the following:

I took another walk around the neighborhood and realized that on this earth as it is—The race is not always to the swift, nor the battle to the strong, nor satisfaction to the wise, nor riches to the smart, nor grace to the learned. Sooner or later, bad luck hits us all. No one can predict misfortune. Like fish caught in a cruel net or birds in a trap, men and women are captured by accidents, evil and sudden.

Ecclesiastes Chapter 9, Verses 11-12

This Biblical message offers excellent takeaways for anyone, especially for justice-impacted people.

My name is Michael Santos, and I founded Prison Professors with the hopes of helping people in jail and prison learn how to self-advocate. Too many people in custody give up hope. They may not belong in prison, but they should never stop working to advocate for liberty.

Sometimes, people going through the system may find it helpful to learn from others who emerged successfully after walking through a similar journey of hardship.

To strive for liberty at the soonest possible time, people may consider a path I learned from leaders. They adhere to a disciplined, deliberate plan when they seek to resolve a challenge. If you want to get the best outcome, consider taking the following steps:

1. Define success as the best possible outcome,

2. Build a plan to go from where you are today to where you want to go,

3. Put priorities in place,

4. Create an accountability metric to measure progress, and

5. Execute the plan every day.

With the message from Ecclesiastes, we have evidence that people have been dealing with unexpected challenges since the beginning of time. No one anticipates spending time in prison. But if a person knows how to prepare a solid release plan, a person may work toward a better outcome.

Every justice-impacted person wants the best possible outcome. To get that outcome, however, a person should prepare and understand how stakeholders view success from the system.

What will our adversaries expect of us?

That question should guide our preparations. It always helped me make better, more deliberate decisions.

LEARN FROM LEADERS:

In one of his influential books on personal leadership, Malcolm Gladwell wrote that a person could become an expert at any task by devoting 10,000 hours of practice. Over 9,500 days, I spent 228,000 hours living as federal prisoner number 16377-004. Throughout that journey, I prepared for the challenges I expected to face.

From the loneliness of a jail cell, I would stare at the wall and anticipate the people I would meet in the future. If they had discretion over my future, I contemplated how I could influence how they perceived me. Like every other justice-impacted person should do, I thought about future case managers, wardens, probation officers, judges, employers, and prospective business partners.

What could I do during my imprisonment to help others see how I responded to problems I created with my criminal behavior rather than the problems that led me to prison?

What tools, tactics, and resources could I create to advocate more effectively through the storms ahead?

In what ways would the tools I developed convert my adversaries into my advocates?

During this era of prison reform, it's more important than ever for justice-impacted people to contemplate such questions. The more thought they give to how they're preparing to overcome challenges, the more effective they will become at advancing prospects for liberty at the soonest possible time.

When I write about this "era of prison reform," I'm referring to several developments:

THE SECOND CHANCE ACT OF 2008:

» President Bush signed this law, which authorized the BOP to allow people to serve up to 12 months of their sentence in a Residential Reentry Center (halfway house). If a person had a sentence of 60 months or longer, the person could serve the final six months in home confinement; if a person had a sentence of fewer than 60 months, the person could serve the last 10% of the sentence in home confinement.

THE FIRST STEP ACT:

» President Trump signed the First Step Act in December of 2018. It's the most significant piece of reform legislation since the Sentence Reform Act of 1987, which introduced the Federal Sentencing Guidelines. As with all reform movements, we can anticipate many rounds of litigation and advocacy. Each ruling will bring clarity to the way that the BOP trains staff members to implement the First Step Act in a uniform way across the country.

THE CARES ACT:

» With the pandemic, President Trump signed an executive order that influenced how the government operated. The attorney general wrote a series of memorandums that mandated the Bureau of Prisons to reduce its prison population by sending appropriate people to serve their sentences in home confinement. President Biden rescinded the CARES Act after the end of the pandemic, but we have significant data from that Act that bolsters the call for reform.

"As of May 27, 2023, BOP had placed 13,204 individuals into home confinement under [the CARES Act]. As of May, just 22 of those people had been returned to prison for committing a new crime."

For original report, see: report by the Niskanen Center

- *https://www.niskanencenter.org/safer-smarter-and-cheaper-the-promise-of-targeted-home-confinement-with-electronic-monitoring/*

Each of the reform movements I mentioned influenced people in federal prison. In common, each reform movement mandated that administrators in the Bureau of Prisons put more emphasis on preparing people for successful, law-abiding lives upon release. **They require staff members to pay close attention to release plans**.

BOP Director Colette Peters published her vision of the "Future state for the BOP:"

Our highly skilled diverse and innovate workforce creates a strong foundation of safety and security, through the principles of humanity and normalcy we develop good neighbors.

Justice-impacted people should understand how administrators measure excellence in a release plan. The National Institute of Justice, the Vera Institute, the Urban Institute, and others publish extensive documentation on release plans. Our team at Prison Professors relies upon that evidence-based documentation, but we also defer to the subject-matter experts we retain.

Those who have access to our subject-matter expert page on Prison Professors may have watched interviews I've done with people who built careers in law enforcement. I've interviewed people who built careers as:

- » Leaders of US probation,
- » The Federal Bureau of Prisons,
- » US District Court Judges, and
- » Prosecuting attorneys.

Each subject-matter expert I interviewed expressed the importance of a release plan. They want to see a record that shows positive on-going efforts for change, showing a person's commitment to preparing for success upon release. They want to see evidence that a person has been thoughtful about risk factors—or triggers—that can lead to recidivism.

To prepare a template and model for others to follow, I relied upon the information I received from Jon Gustin. Jon retired from the Bureau of Prisons in 2022 after 24 years of service. When he retired, Jon held the position of Administrator over Residential Reentry Centers (RRCs) that the Bureau of Prisons relied upon across America. We wanted to use the same reliable information that administrators use to create a template justice-impacted people could follow.

During the 26 years that I served in prison (between 1987 and 2013), administrators frequently told me, "We don't care anything about your life after you finish your sentence. We only care about the security of the institution." Administrators locked me in segregation or transferred me to prisons across state lines for doing the same things that the First Step Act now encourages people to do.

A release plan guided my adjustment. By documenting the journey and memorializing the accomplishments I made, I succeeded in overcoming many of the obstacles that complicate life for so many people in prison.

Since completing my obligation to the Bureau of Prisons on August 12, 2013, the arc of justice has bent toward reform, as evidenced by the First Step Act. I will work to bring more reforms, understanding that advocacy takes time and coalitions.

We invite all justice-impacted people to become a part of this coalition. To stand out, and bring attention to the "extraordinary and compelling" adjustments they engineer, I highly recommend that they memorialize each step of their journey. To help, our nonprofit, Prison Professors Charitable Corporation, created PrisonProfessorsTalent.com, which we'll elaborate on in the pages to follow.

At Prison Professors, our team strives to show people how to succeed despite the challenges that they will face. They should expect obstacles and difficulties. They should persevere, always focusing on steps they can take to convert adversaries into advocates.

Any person going into the system should learn to self-advocate. Staff members in the BOP do not respond favorably to people who claim entitlement to benefits or privileges. People help themselves when they can show a sustained record of participating in positive programs. A good record becomes a tool for self-advocacy. And transparency becomes a tool for self-advocacy.

Staff members in the Bureau of Prisons have enormous discretion. For that reason, each person should document efforts toward personal development. They should communicate in a positive and respectful manner. Each person must persevere through the challenges ahead.

I never ask anyone to do anything that I didn't do.

The lessons I learned from prison—and my release plan—helped me launch several ventures upon my release. The practice of documenting my journey opened many opportunities. Those who've read *Earning Freedom: Conquering a 45-Year Prison Term* know that I prepared my "release plan" while awaiting my sentence from a solitary cell of the Pierce County Jail.

After reading *The Crito*, a short book describing Socrates' time in jail, I learned how to stop thinking about my current problems and begin thinking about the broader community.

> » What steps could I take to reconcile with society?
>
> » How could I positively influence the way that others perceived me?
>
> » What plans could I make to advance possibilities for a second chance at life?

Those kinds of open-ended questions influenced my release plan. The sooner a person begins preparing a release plan, the more robust that plan will become.

DYNAMIC PLANS:

People who craft release plans should consider them dynamic documents. In other words, they should evolve over time. This course provides a start for the plan. But it should continue to evolve. A person should use the same principles that we teach in our course: Preparing for Success after Prison.

THAT COURSE TEACHES PEOPLE TO FOLLOW TEN STEPS:

Step 1: Success
» Define success as the best possible outcome.

Step 2: Goals
» Set clear goals that align with your definition of success.

Step 3: Attitude
» Move forward with a 100 percent commitment.

Step 4: Aspiration
» Aspire to something more than the current crisis.

Step 5: Action
» Act in ways that reflect your commitment to success.

Step 6: Accountability
» Measure progress with clear accountability metrics.

Step 7: Awareness
» Keep your head in the game, staying aware of opportunities to create or seize, and making others aware of your progress.

Step 8: Authenticity
» Be authentic, creating tools, tactics, and resources to advance the plan, making adjustments as necessary.

Step 9: Achievement
» Celebrate the small achievements, because they lead to new opportunities.

Step 10: Appreciation
» Live in gratitude, appreciating the benefits that come your way.

We encourage all participants to use our new platform to memorialize their journey. To get started, visit PrisonProfessorsTalent.com. You'll see that we invite people to show their the progress toward advancing their release plans. Take the following steps:

Step 1: Send an email to our interns
» Send an email to Interns@PrisonProfessorsTalent.com

Step 2: Provide your information
» Send identifying information that includes:

» Your name
» Your prison registration number
» The institution where you'll serve the sentence
» The mailing address for the institution
» Your sentence length
» The date of your surrender
» Your projected release date

(If you don't have the information above, you can update the profile later)

Step 3: Write your Bio
» Write a bio to help people learn more about your life.
» If you'd like to feature your image on your profile, ask a family member or friend to send a digital image.
» Write additional biographies as your release evolves.

Step 4: Journal to show your commmitment to excellence
» Start writing a journal, showing how you're preparing for success upon release.
» Flesh out your journal to show the incremental progress you're making.

Step 5: Write book reports
» Write book reports for every book that you read.
» Show your commitment to self-directed learning.

Step 6: Show the evolution of your release plan
» Write each version of your release plan.

Step 7: Build your tribe
» Start building your tribe by helping others advance their prospects for success.

When more people participate in Prison Professors Talent, we strengthen our message for reform.

Although I am confident that the following lessons will help any justice-impacted person, my area of expertise and experience lies with the federal system. Regardless of where a person serves time, a release plan will influence a person's ability to navigate the pathway toward the soonest possible release date. Indeed, many prison reform movements emphasize the importance of a release plan.

Please consider the following as a self-directed template. We encourage participants in our course to use what they deem appropriate and to craft their release plan.

With hopes of proving worthy of your trust, we offer this plan as a starting point. It's not perfect because it needs your input. Following the template, I offer an example of how I would have used it to influence stakeholders that had discretion over my life.

With best wishes for the success of all participants, I speak for every member of our team at Prison Professors in wishing you success.

Sincerely,
Michael Santos
PrisonProfessors.com

PRISONPROFESSORSTALENT: IMAGES

Since many members of the Prison Professors community are in prison, they will not have access to the internet. They will not see our platform, and may not fully grasp how building a profile can assist their preparations for release. To give them a better idea of how to develop a profile, and how to use it, we include these images. We encourage participants to have family members and friends to visit the live website to get the full experience.

HOME PAGE (1)

Culture (2)
» Interior page to emphasize Director Peters' statement about the agency's mission of working to create good neighbors rather than good inmates.

Planning (3)
» Interior page to show how the importance of creating a plan at the start of a journey, and building upon the plan to show incremental progress and commitment to excellence.

Employment (4)
» Interior page to show our efforts to build relationships with employers who may offer income opportunities for people who use time in prison to prepare for success upon release.

Halim Flowers (5)
» Interior page highlighting the inspiring story of Halim Flowers. Despite going to prison at 16, with a double-life sentence, Halim memorialied his release plan, then used it to self-advocate and leverage his plan to freedom and success upon release.

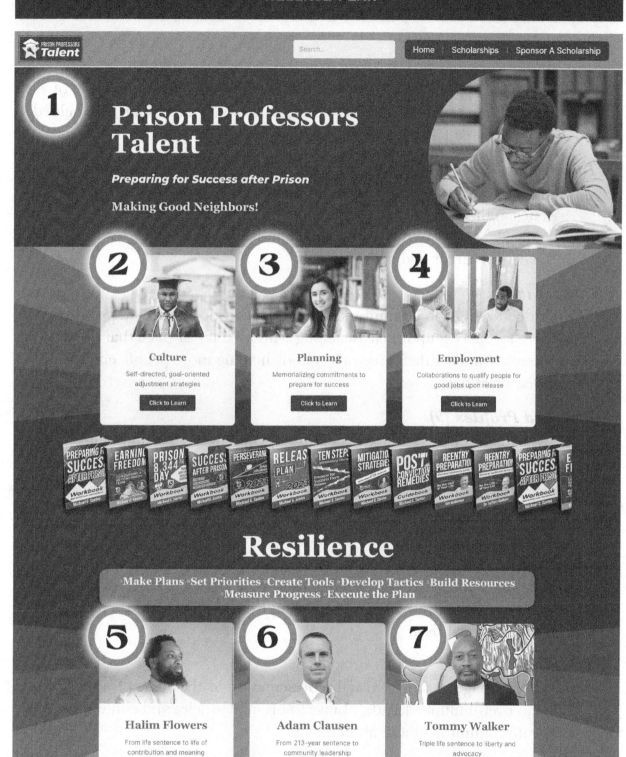

Prison Professors Talent

Preparing for Success after Prison

Making Good Neighbors!

Culture
Self-directed, goal-oriented adjustment strategies

Click to Learn

Planning
Memorializing commitments to prepare for success

Click to Learn

Employment
Collaborations to qualify people for good jobs upon release

Click to Learn

Resilience

◦Make Plans ◦Set Priorities ◦Create Tools ◦Develop Tactics ◦Build Resources ◦Measure Progress ◦Execute the Plan

Halim Flowers
From life sentence to life of contribution and meaning

Click Here

Adam Clausen
From 213-year sentence to community leadership

Click Here

Tommy Walker
Triple life sentence to liberty and advocacy

Click Here

Being the Change we

Adam Clauson (6)

» Interior page featuring Adam Clauson, who once served a 213-year prison term. With an effective release plan, and ample documentation of his preparation for success upon release, Adam built a coalition that helped him persuade a federal judge to grant him liberty.

Tommy Walker (7)

» Interior page to profile Tommy Walker, who once served a triple-life sentence at the United States Penitentiary, Lewisburg. Tommy's release plan evolved, and he used it to persuade a judge to release him and to build a successful career upon release.

Impact (8)

» Video to show our commitment to helping justice-impacted people prepare for success upon release, along with an interior page that shows how we're advancing the Director's goal of helping more people emerge as good neighbors.

Featured Profiles (9)

» Dynamic feature to bring attention to people who commit to developing their release plans. The more people publish about their commitment to excellence, with updated bios, journal entries, book reports, or evolving release plans, the more points they earn toward being featured on the home page. Features link back to the individual's profile page.

Institutions (10)

» Graphical image to show the institutions where we're currently partnering to introduce our courses, including Release Plans and Preparing for Success after Prison

Timeline (11)

» Interior page to show a visual representation of the value of a release plan over multiple decades. Links to original articles and content demonstrate commitment and authenticity.

8

Being the Change we Want to See

The First Step Act encourages and incentivizes people to pursue excellence while they serve their sanctions. Sponsor a student. Learn how we're building coalitions with administrators, employers, citizens, and people inside to end intergenerational cycles of recidivism. We offer daily lessons to prepare more people for success upon release.

See our Impact: Institutions and People we Serve

Feature Students

9 ♜ ♜ ♜

Melinda Bixler
FDC Philadelphia
● ● ●

On June 20, 2023, I turned 51 years old. It was uneventful, absent from any celebration. Primarily because I'm just sisters, brothers, and me the importance of education...

Choon Yong
USP Atwater
● ● ●

My Name is Yong Choon Foo (Keith). I was born in Malaysia on October 13, 1955. My parents impressed upon my verse today:
Mark 7:18-20 (Paraphrasing)...

Jeffrey Piecka
USP Thomson
● ● ●

As part of my daily routine of bettering myself physically, mentally, and spiritually, I came across this Bible convicted me, and a judge sentenced me to serve 45 years in prison...

● ● ● ●

10 ## Contributing to Excellence at:

MCC Chicago MCFP Springfield FCC Florence FCI Englewood FMC Rochester

FPC Duluth USP Marion North Kern State Prison USP Leavenworth FCI Pekin

USP Thomson FCC Terre Haute Donovan Correctional Pelican Bay State Prison

FPC Yankton FCI Sandstone Avenal State Prison Wasco State Prison Folsom

Calipatria State Prison Centinela State Prison Corcoran State Prison FCI Milan

CCWF Women's Prison California Correctional Pleasant Valley State Prison

Institute for Men High Desert State Prison Ironwood State Prison FCI Waseca

Kern Valley State Prison Mule Creek State Prison FCI Greenville FCI Oxford

11

Prison to PhD

View Timeline

PRISON PROFESSORS **Talent**

Navigation: Home (12)
» Link that leads visitors back to the home page.

Navigation: Scholarships (13)
» Link that profiles the scholarships we're offering
» Links that show our commitment to matching institutional orders
» Links that show our roster of partiipants.

Navigation: Sponsor (14)
» Interior page to show process for sponsoring justice-impacted people.

PERSONAL PROFILE (15):
» Our inters will open a personal profile for any person who sends an invite to Interns@PrisonProfessorsTalent.com. Participants may continue to send updated information to show how they're preparing for success upon release. They may use their profile as a central location to show their commitment to excellence, with a well-developed release plan that matured over time.

Image (16)
» Although not necessary, participants may choose to feature a headshot, or image, in an effort to build rapport and develop a relationship with potential advocates.

Identifying Information (17)
» Our interns will build a profile for those who reach out. We will provide contact information that helps potential advocates get a snapshot of the person, and know how to connect. We're investing to create an RSS feed, or subscription service that will automatically update subscribers with news on when the individual posts something new, provided that subscribers want to receive such updates.

Bio (18)
» Participants should write a biography, or series of biographies. The biography will help an individual begin to restore a reputation, helping readers get more context into why the person is in prison, and the commitment he is making to prepare for success upon release.

Journal Entries (19)
» Participants may journal to show the self-directed steps to prepare for success upon release. Show the investment in personal development to build support and to convert adversaries into advocates.

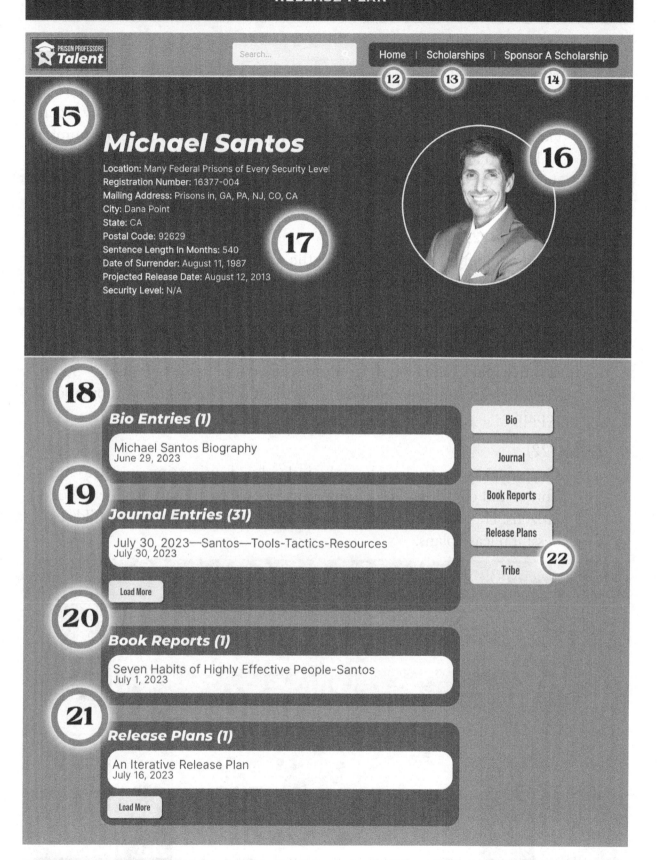

PRISON PROFESSORS
Talent

Search...

Home | Scholarships | Sponsor A Scholarship

12   13   14

15

Michael Santos

Location: Many Federal Prisons of Every Security Level
Registration Number: 16377-004
Mailing Address: Prisons in, GA, PA, NJ, CO, CA
City: Dana Point
State: CA
Postal Code: 92629
Sentence Length In Months: 540
Date of Surrender: August 11, 1987
Projected Release Date: August 12, 2013
Security Level: N/A

16

17

18

Bio Entries (1)

Michael Santos Biography
June 29, 2023

19

Journal Entries (31)

July 30, 2023—Santos—Tools-Tactics-Resources
July 30, 2023

Load More

20

Book Reports (1)

Seven Habits of Highly Effective People-Santos
July 1, 2023

21

Release Plans (1)

An Iterative Release Plan
July 16, 2023

Load More

Bio

Journal

Book Reports

Release Plans

Tribe

22

PRISON PROFESSORS
Talent

Book Reports (20)

» Our courses urge participants to show their commitment to self-directed learning. Regardless of what goes on an institution, a person can start sowing seeds to prepare for the collateral consequences that follow a conviction. We urge people to write book reports to memorialize the number of books read, the lessons learned, and the way that reading will contribute to success upon release. Those book reports become an asset that a person can use to convert adversaries into advocates.

Release Plans (21)

» Build an initial release plan, using the template we include. Then, develop the release plan to show commitment to excellence. Each person should use discretion when developing a release plan, with an understanding that it can help a person self-advocate for a higher-level of liberty at various stages of the journey, including: 1) preparing before sentencing, 2) administrative relief in prison, 3) freedom while in the halfway house, 4) Supervised Release, and potential early termination, 5) career and reputational repair.

Tribe (22)

» Graphical image to show how the individual is using time inside to recalibrate and contribute to helping more people to prepare for life as good citizens. Highlight the number of people you're mentoring to build successful release plans.

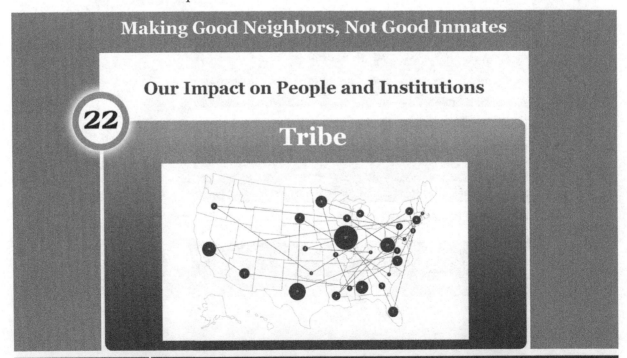

Student Profiles Built
187
Our team has built profiles for these students

July

Student Profiles to Build
7
Students waiting for our team to build profiles

Growth
98%

Last month   Today

Student Journal Entries
170
Number of journal entries students have submitted

1-8   9-16   17-23   24-31

Student Bio Entries
71
Number of biographies that students have submitted.

Student Bios	Weekly
+43	
+28	

Student Release Plans
3
Number of release plans students have submitted.

Student Book Reports
38
Number of book reports students have submitted.

Expense Details

	USP Florence	$10,564.40
	FCI Waseca	$6,688.50
	FCI Florence	$3,430.00
	MCC Chicago	$3,430.00
	USP Leavenworth	$3,430.00
	Individual Book Donations Many Courses	$5,635.00

Books we've donated
1,475
Books we've donated to students who are preparing for success upon release

Value of books that we've donated to justice-impacted students
$5,635
Our nonprofit supports institutions by matching the amount they purchase.

Value of books that we've donated to match institutional purchases
$42,703.5
Our nonprofit supports institutions by matching the amount they purchase.

Total Value of books that we've donated to institutions and justice-impacted students
$48,338.5
Our nonprofit supports institutions by matching the amount they purchase.

Income Rate

$0 $50k $100k

PRISON PROFESSORS
Talent

TOOLS / TACTICS / RESOURCES:

Developing tools, tactics, and resources helped me prepare for success while I served 26 years in prison. The strategy helped me to recalibrate and build businesses during my first decade in liberty. I continue using the technique to overcome opposition to my advocacy efforts.

The Release Plan workbook is a tactic, a part of my overall strategy to advocate for reforms. I will use this resource to build coalitions. Those coalitions will help me to persuade administrators and legislators to change laws and policies. Those changes should incentivize a pursuit of excellence.

INCENTIVIZE EXCELLENCE:

If we want more people to leave prison as good neighbors rather than good inmates, we must follow the same principles that define America—we incentivize excellence. We create systems that encourage people to work hard.

Although I want to see those changes, many people oppose my vision. They detest talk of reforms that allow people to work toward earning freedom. I face such resistance routinely, and I need a tool to overcome those objections.

Our new platform, Prison Professors Talent, will profile thousands of people who commit to preparing for success after prison. If I can highlight those people, I'll have a resource to persuade taxpayers, employers, administrators, and legislators on the value of such reforms.

> *"If we can help other people get what they want, we can get every-thing we want."*
>
> *Zig Zigler*

People in prison do not know the challenges or opposition we face when we advocate for reforms that include:

» Work release programs,

» Expanded use of furloughs,

» Access to Compassionate release,

» Reinstatement of the US Parole Commission.

Understandably, people in prison miss their families and their liberty. They do not fully grasp the implications of what follows when a federal judge says: "I sentence you to the custody of the Attorney General." At that moment, the person transitions from the judicial to the executive branch of government. Administrators in the Bureau of Prisons will carry out the judge's order.

The Code of Federal Regulations gives The Bureau of Prisons considerable discretion. Congress has vested the agency with the power to determine where a person serves a sentence. Thanks to policies during the COVID pandemic, we have evidence that the Bureau of Prisons can manage people more effectively in home-confinement-type settings than in a federal prison.

> *"As of May 27, 2023, BOP had placed 13,204 individuals into home confinement under [the CARES Act]. As of May, just 22 of those people had been returned to prison for committing a new crime."*

With Prison Professors Talent, we'll have a new resource to further our advocacy. From this Release Plan workbook, we hope more people in prison will learn how to build effective release plans and memorialize their commitment to excellence.

By building their profiles and documenting their pursuit of excellence, participants will not only become part of the coalition working to advocate for reform, but they'll also develop a personal resource. They can use it as an asset to convert adversaries into advocates, and to open more opportunities that will advance prospects for success upon release. This strategy positioned me for success in prison and beyond. It led to higher income levels, and a higher level of liberty than I would have had otherwise.

In our books, I show the relationship between an evolving release plan and success upon release. I also show the failure that follows for people who do not build effective release plans.

For example, consider the case of Larry Levine, a person who attempted to persuade a federal judge to grant early termination to his term of Supervised Release, but failed. In the published opinion, the federal judge said:

> *"Defendant has not demonstrated a significant change to warrant early termination….A defendant should not obtain early release for doing what is already legally required to do. Courts have generally found that a showing of an exceptional circumstance beyond mere compliance is needed. Here, the Court finds that Defendant has not*

made any showing of an exceptional circumstance beyond mere compliance with the terms of his supervised release."

The Honorable Ronald S.W. Lew, Senior U.S. District Court Judge
United States of America v. Lawrence Jay Levine

If you're striving for excellence and you want to engineer a pathway that will lead to a better outcome, start preparing now.

Show why you're worthy of relief. Be exceptional and compelling.

Federal Bureau of Prisons

A-Z Topics • Site Map • FOIA

Search bop.gov

| Home | About Us | Inmates | Locations | Careers | Business | Resources | Contact Us |

Reentry Success

Education and Reentry Programming: Keys to Success

Updated 12:30 PM , June 20, 2023

(BOP) - Michael Santos was a young man who made a terrible mistake and learned the hard lesson that life is not like the movies and actions have consequences. Today, he is a productive, law-abiding citizen-a university professor, prison consultant, motivational speaker, life coach, and an advocate for criminal justice reform. He also developed an online course titled, "Preparing for Success after Prison," which is now offered by the National Institute of Corrections (NIC).

While serving a 26-year sentence, Mr. Santos used his time in prison to transform his life for the better. He took advantage of Bureau of Prisons (BOP) reentry programming and enrolled in college courses. He earned his bachelor's and master's degree; and he became a prolific writer, publishing several books and articles about prison life and reform. Since his release in 2013, Santos has shared his story and insights with various audiences. During a recent American Correctional Association (ACA) conference, NIC Director (A) Dr. Alix McLearen, and Andre Matevousian, Regional Director (RD) of the North Central Region, noted Santos' inspiring presentation. As a result, RD Matevousian encouraged the Wardens in his region to welcome Santos into their institutions to share his empowering story about how reentry programming can transform lives.

Headline News Articles

- Pell Grants Restores Possibilities for Incarcerated People
- Bold Steps for Correctional Excellence
- Danbury Hosts Stakeholder Tour
- Mission Change for FCI Oxford Announced
- More BOP News

About Us
About Our Agency
About Our Facilities
Historical Information
Statistics

Inmates
Find an Inmate
First Step Act
Communications
Custody & Care
Visiting
Report a Concern

Locations
List of our Facilities
Map of our Locations
Search for a Facility

Careers
Life at the BOP
Explore Opportunities
Current Openings
Application Process
Our Hiring Process

Business
Acquisitions
Solicitations & Awards
Reentry Contracting

Resources
Policy & Forms
News Stories
Press Releases
Publications
Research & Reports

Resources For ...
Victims & Witnesses
Employees
Volunteers
Former Inmates
Media Reps

 PRISON PROFESSORS Talent

RELEASE PLAN TEMPLATE

Name

Registration Number

Prison Location

Release Plan

Date

INTRODUCTORY OPENING:

In this section, participants should write an opening letter that shows the logic behind their release plan. A person who prepares well will have researched the best-practice for serving a sentence. One logical place to begin would be the website of the Bureau of Prisons.

For longer than a month, beginning on June 2023, the Bureau of Prisons reserved its home page to highlight the importance of preparing for success after prison. Anyone can see that article with the following link:

» Education and Reentry Programming: Keys to Success

» Reentry Success

» https://www.bop.gov/resources/news/20230620_reentry_success.jsp

That article emphasized the importance of building good release plans. A good release plan begins with preparation.

Each person should write an introduction that details their commitment to building a release plan that followed the "Keys to Success" as the BOP highlighted.

The sample release plan that follows in the next section offers a templated letter that participants may modify to suit their needs. We recommend including the following information:

1. Identifying Information	7. Community Support
2. Images	8. Medical Prescriptions
3. Projected Release Planning	9. Financial Obligations
4. Background	10. Risk and Needs Assessment
5. My Conviction	11. Personal Plan
6. Making Amends	12. Advisors

SECTION 1: IDENTIFYING INFORMATION:

- » Name
- » Date of Birth:
- » Today's Date:
- » Previous versions
- » Sentence Length:
- » Surrender Date and Location:
- » Community phone number:
- » Community email:

SECTION 2: IMAGE VALIDATION

- » Driver's license image:
- » Social security card image:
- » High School Diploma image:
- » Birth certificate image:

» Proof of US Citizenship (if not a natural-born citizen)

» Insurance Card image:

» (Include images of documents that will help administrators)

SECTION 3: PROJECTED RELEASE PLANNING:

Explain the steps you took to begin building your plan. Help administrators understand what prompted you to build this plan, how you intend to use the plan, and how you will continue to develop the plan.

Strive to show that you've put considerable thought into preparing for your success upon release. We would recommend that you create a projected release date, citing your qualification for potential credits related to:

» Good Conduct Time

» Earned Time Credit

» Residential Drug Abuse Program

SECTION 4: BACKGROUND:

When building a release plan, remember that you're not writing for the people you love or the people who love you. You're creating this plan for stakeholders of the criminal justice system. Their job descriptions require that they carry out the order of the judge.

Remember when a judge imposes a prison term, he says:

With the power vested in me, I sentence you to the custody of the Attorney General for …. Months.

The people who carry out the sentence align themselves with the judge's order. That is their job. Do not think of them as nurses or doctors to help ease your way through challenging complications. Instead, it would be wise to remember that they go through training, and their training requires that they abide by policies and procedures.

The more a person understands the challenges ahead, the better a person can prepare a release plan.

Considering the people who will have discretion over liberty, we think it best for each person to begin by providing background information. Present yourself in a way that will humanize you. Write between 500 and 750 words that show who you are and how you got here. Explain the influences that led to your current predicament.

Then get into the conviction.

SECTION 5: MY CONVICTION:

Stakeholders will have ample documentation that the government presented about the crime. Use this section to put the crime into context. Help your reader get to know you as a person, and not as a registration number.

Describe why you're more than the criminal past.

I found that I could disarm people by explaining the lessons that I learned from leaders.

If guilty of the crime:

 » Show that you understand the gravity of the crime,

 » Identify with the victims,

 » Explain the influences that to the crime,

 » Describe your commitment to reconciliation.

If not guilty of the crime:

 » Consider the influences that led you here,

 » Respect the verdict and process, including guidance from counsel,

 » Find analogies that will make your story more plausible,

 » Present your story in a manner that does not evoke animosity, or leave others with the impression that you're illogical.

SECTION 6: MAKING AMENDS

This section should help your reader see that you've learned from this experience. Always write for the stakeholders you want to influence. To create opportunities for a better outcome, consider that people who respect law and social norms will have enormous influence over your life.

Anticipate that people will say that you're only sorry because you got caught. Build a release plan that will disarm adversaries. Consider steps you can take to convert them into adversaries.

Your pathway should consider the instrument that prosecutors used to bring charges. In my case, a prosecutor convened a grand jury. Members of the grand jury returned an indictment stated United States of America v. Michael Santos, charging me with serious crimes that exposed me to life in prison. After a trial, a jury convicted me of all counts, exposing me to life in prison. My judge sentenced me to 45 years.

Every person's release plan should take facts into account. I could not change the past, but stakeholders would always judge me for the events that led to my conviction.

Each person should design the release plan to take those factors into account. Use this section to elicit empathy and support, building a case that is bigger than the personal story. Reconcile with society and build support to write the next chapter of your life.

SECTION 7: COMMUNITY SUPPORT

The release plan should show that a person has a support network. That support group should express commitment to helping the individual make the transition into society.

At the very least, cite your housing plans:

» Where will you live?

» Who will live with you?

» What challenges will you face in living there?

» Who will assist you with your living plans?

Always consider the stakeholder, the audience for this release plan. Many people who work in the criminal justice system have a cynical view of justice-impacted people. High recidivism rates influence their perceptions, and they may be reluctant to believe that a person in prison has a support system in place to help the individual triumph over the collateral consequences of a conviction.

To address such factors, the release plan should validate that a person has community support. Each expression of support should include the writer's contact information, showing a commitment to transparency.

Potential Problems to Address:

» If you have not secured housing, what options are you considering?

» How will you prepare for permanent housing?

SECTION 8: MEDICAL PRESCRIPTIONS / SUBSTANCE ABUSE

If you take prescriptions, or struggle with medical complications, use this section to record that information.

People with a history of substance abuse or alcoholism may want to list that information here, too. By providing this information, a person may qualify for programs to treat the complication.

Although each person must decide the right course of action to take, transparency has always helped me.

SECTION 9: FINANCIAL OBLIGATIONS

Many times, a federal judge imposes a financial sanction. That sanction may be a criminal fine or a restitution order. Either way, if the judge imposed a fine, address that matter in the release plan. Stakeholders will want to see that you're dealing with the fine responsibly.

While serving time in the Bureau of Prisons, staff members will expect a person to comply with the Financial Responsibility Program (FRP). We encourage people to understand that program before they surrender:

» https://prisonprofessors.com/understanding-the-frp-program/

Although the Program Statement is extensive, it's worth reading because it helps participants understand the relationship between participating in the FRP program, and qualification for programs that can advance release dates.

» In the federal system, the United States has 20 years to collect on a fine. We published an article on this topic, including links to the law:

https://prisonprofessors.com/what-should-i-know-about-restitution-or-ders-for-white-collar-crime/

» https://www.law.cornell.edu/uscode/text/18/3613

"The liability to pay a fine shall terminate the later of 20 years from the entry of judgment or 20 years after the release from imprisonment of the person fine, or upon the death of the individual fined."

Title 18 U.S. Code § 3613 - Civil remedies for satisfaction of an unpaid fine

SECTION 10: RISK AND NEEDS ASSESSMENT

The First Step Act changed the mandate of the Bureau of Prisons. It is the most significant reform of the prison system in longer than three decades. President Trump signed the legislation in 2018, yet because of the way that the law would force the Bureau of Prisons to change, Congress anticipated rolling the law out over several year.

One significant change in the law included a mechanism that could accelerate release dates for people who qualified. Congress published the crimes that would not qualify for Earned Time Credits. The following link shows the "disqualifying offenses."

» https://www.bop.gov/resources/fsa/time_credits_disqualifying_offenses.jsp

If a person does not have a disqualifying offense, the person shall receive Earned Time Credits as follows:

A prisoner shall earn ten days of time credits for every 30 days of successful participation in programs.

If the BOP risk-assessment shows that the person has been a minimum- or low-risk of recidivating after two consecutive assessments, the person will receive an additional five days of time credits.

Conservatively, a person who qualifies might anticipate earning ten days of time credit during the first seven months of confinement, and 15 days of time credit after the person receives the second team meeting.

We encourage participants to work through the risk assessment before surrendering. If a person knows how he or she will score on a risk assessment, a person is in a better position to self-advocate.

- » Male PATTERN Tool
- » Female PATTERN Tool
- » PATTERN Violent Offense Codes
- » Male and Female Cut Points

SECTION 11: PERSONAL PLAN

This section might define your vision statement. No one can change the past, but we all can sow seeds for a brighter future. To create a plan, we must have a clear understanding of what we're striving to build. Use this section to show that you've considered your strengths, weaknesses, opportunities, and threats.

To live as the CEO of your life, our courses recommend that each person begins by defining success. To paraphrase the Cheshire Cat from Alice in Wonderland:

If a person doesn't know where he is going, any road will take him there.

Many people face challenges after prison for the same reasons that businesses frequently fail: they do not have a plan.

To succeed, take the following steps:

- » Define success,
- » Create a plan,
- » Set priorities,
- » Develop tools, tactics, and resources,
- » Measure progress with daily accountability metrics,
- » Modify the plan as necessary, and
- » Execute the plan every day.

SECTION 12: ADVISORS

People who succeed surround themselves with advisors. Describe the people who advised you in creating your plan. Commit to them and invite them to become your accountability partners.

Show deference to the Unit Team and staff members in prison. Seek their guidance and follow their advice.

SAMPLE RELEASE PLAN:

Michael Sample
Registration Number xxxxx-xxx
Federal Prison Name
Release Plan

July xx, 20xx

Dear Unit Team:

Before surrendering, I researched the best practice for serving time in federal prison. From that research, I found the Bureau of Prisons' home page, which profiled an article:

» Education and Reentry Programming
» Keys to Success
» https://www.bop.gov/resources/news/20230620_reentry_success.jsp

The article emphasized the importance of building good release plan and suggested that a good release plan begins with preparation. It led me to participate in courses and to learn as much as possible. As I studied the information, I learned about the role of the Unit Team in the Bureau of Prisons and the importance of developing a comprehensive release plan.

Based on what I learned, I created this plan to guide me through the journey, and to prepare for a successful outcome from every aspect of this system, including imprisonment, home confinement, and supervised release.

I pleaded guilty, and I accept responsibility for my mistakes. I am ashamed of my actions that brought me here, but I know that remorse alone cannot make amends for my crime. With my Unit Team's guidance and the accountability of my loved ones, I will remain committed to making this time productive, reconciling with society, and strengthening relationships with my family.

I developed my release plan as an accountability tool that describes my self-directed pathway to prepare for the best outcomes after my release. I will continue updating and expanding the document as I meet milestones on my journey and set new goals consistent with my commitments.

The plan includes the following information:

1. Identifying Information	7. Community Support
2. Images	8. Medical Prescriptions
3. Projected Release Planning	9. Financial Obligations
4. Background	10. Risk and Needs Assessment
5. My Conviction	11. Personal Plan
6. Making Amends	12. Advisors

I hope the Unit Team finds this plan helpful in guiding me back to my family and community as soon as possible.

IDENTIFYING INFORMATION:

» Name: My name is Michael Sample and my Prison Registration Number is XXXXX-XXX.

» Date of Birth: I was born on September 11, 1980, and I am 42 years old.

» Today's Date: I began writing this release plan on June 06, 2023

» Sentence Length: US District Court Judge Richard D. Walker, from the District of Kansas, sentenced me to serve a sentence of 30-months, followed by two years of Supervised Release.

» Surrender Date and Location: Based on information my attorney provided, I anticipate surrendering to the Federal Prison Camp in Maryland on July 31, 2023.

» My community phone number: (xxx) xxx-xxxx

» My community Email: MichaelSample@gmail.com

IMAGES:

To provide my Unit Team with validating information, on the final page of this document, I attach pages that include images from the following identifying documents:

- » Driver's License: Valid driver's license from the state of Kansas

- » High School Diploma: Copy of my diploma from Best High School, in Wichita

- » Bachelor's Degree: Copy of my bachelor's degree from Kansas State University

- » Master's Degree: Copy of my master's degree from Kansas State University

- » VA card: Copy of my card from the Veterans Administration

- » Birth Certificate: Copy of my birth certificate

- » Social Security Card: Copy of my Social Security Card

PROJECTED RELEASE PLANNING:

Many years of schooling and military service have impressed upon me the importance of planning. We must plan if we want to work toward the best possible outcome.

To that end, I began studying the Bureau of Prisons' website. That website led me to a series of links that showed the importance of release plans. Through that research, I learned about the First Step Act and other BOP policies. It is my understanding that good behavior and program participation can influence an earlier transition to home confinement.

With guidance from my Unit Team, I hope to advance as an excellent candidate for consideration of early transition to home confinement.

Various BOP Program Statements helped me understand how I can earn additional credits toward the sentence my judge imposed. I learned that if I avoid disciplinary infractions, my Unit Team will award Good Conduct Time credits that

amounts to 15% of the term my judge imposed. With my sentence of 30 months, I anticipate receiving credit of 4.5 months.

According to my understanding, these credits leave me with a potential adjusted sentence of approximately 25.5 months.

In addition to the Good Conduct Time credits, if I comply with specific requirements, I may also earn "Time Credits," in accordance with the First Step Act (FSA). Before qualifying for those FSA credits, I have a responsibility to complete a survey once I surrender to prison. My responses to questions on that survey will help my Unit Team assess my risk of recidivating with a PATTERN score.

The BOP's website includes the survey questions for the PATTERN Risk Assessment:

> » https://www.bop.gov/inmates/fsa/pattern.jsp

I began working through those questions independently. Based on what I learned, I anticipate that my Unit Team will agree that my PATTERN score will show me as a person with a "minimum" risk of recidivating.

Initial Classification: According to a policy statement that I read on the BOP's website, I understand that my Unit Team will meet with me for an Initial Unit Team meeting within 30 days of my surrender. During that Initial Classification, I anticipate that my Unit Team will agree that I am at a "minimum" risk of recidivating.

I will participate in all programs that my Unit Team recommends.

If I am accurate, I anticipate that during each of my first six months in confinement, I will receive ten days of Earned Time credit.

Program Review: The BOP website tells me that after six months, I will have another Unit Team meeting, known as a Program Review. During that Program Review, I anticipate that my Unit Team will conclude that I remain at a minimum risk of recidivating.

After two consecutive team meetings, I anticipate that my Unit Team will conclude that my PATTERN Risk Assessment will continue to show a minimum risk of recidivating. Since I will complete all programs that my Unit Team recommends, I should begin to receive 15 days of Earned Time Credit each month for the remainder of my sentence.

Using those parameters, I projected the potential time that I will serve in prison before I become eligible to transition to home confinement.

> » Sentence my judge imposed: 30 months.

> » Good Conduct Time: Approximately 4.5 months, for adjusted sentence of approximately 25.5 months.

> » FSA Earned Time Credit: 10 days per month for my first six months, and 15 days per month going forward.

I understand that I will serve a portion of that time in the XXXXX Federal Prison Camp.

I understand that, at the discretion of my Unit Team, I may qualify to serve a portion of my term in a Residential Reentry Center (Halfway House) or on home confinement.

With this plan, I hope that my Unit Team will learn more about the steps I intend to take to advance my candidacy for early placement on home confinement.

If my projections are accurate, after factoring in Good Conduct Time and Earned Time Credits, I anticipate owing the Bureau of Prisons approximately 15 months. For reasons that I explain with this plan, I am hopeful that the Bureau of Prisons will consider me a candidate for transition to a Residential Reentry Center at the earliest possible time.

I seek guidance from my Unit Team to help me understand steps I can take to qualify for maximum placement on home confinement, in accordance with what I read about the First Step Act.

BACKGROUND:

I am ashamed to write this document. My parents did not raise me to be a criminal, and I knew better than to engage in the type of conduct that could lead to problems with the law. Although I know that my Unit Team will have a presentence investigation report and other documents that describe my crime, I thought it might be helpful for me to offer more insight, to reveal who I am as a human being.

I grew up in Wichita Kansas, the second child of a loving family. My father devoted his entire career to government service, and my mother worked as a nurse. We lived in a modest house in a crime-free neighborhood. Through my adolescence, our parents emphasized the importance of education and living as good citizens.

I tried to live up to their expectations. In this instance, I failed them. I failed my family and I failed myself.

As a young man, I aspired to work in the financial sector. I applied myself in high school and earned good grades. After graduating from high school, I began my university studies with a focus on economics. In four years, I earned a degree in economics. The university considered my grades sufficiently good enough to transition into the business school, and I earned a master's degree in business.

With hopes of building a career in finance, I accepted a job with a major brokerage house. Within a few months, I earned the necessary licenses to build a career as a financial advisor. In that role, I built relationships with many researchers. They advised me on what their research revealed. I learned about the advance orders companies received and I learned about shipments in the pipeline. That research was not public information, but I understood that it could give me a competitive advantage.

I am ashamed to admit that I breached trust and used that information to profit unfairly. I also passed along that information to others, and they also profited from the information I provided.

MY CRIME:

When I studied for the licensing exams that allowed me to build my career, I went through many lessons on ethics. I understood securities laws and the importance of maintaining the financial integrity of the US markets. The markets will not function if people do not have trust. For that reason, laws exist to further fairness in the markets and to prevent trading on material, non-public information.

When presented with information that had not yet been shared with the public, I knew that I had an advantage. Thinking that I could avoid detection, I orchestrated a series of transactions that benefited my personal account. I also passed

along that information to others, and they also traded on that non-public information. Or actions violated the law.

I compounded my crimes by masquerading my income on my tax returns. A government investigation led to the discovery of my brokerage account. With that information, prosecutors conveyed a grand jury. An indictment for securities fraud followed.

I pleaded guilty to those charges and cooperated fully with investigators.

MAKING AMENDS:

I understand my duty and responsibility to work toward making things right. While I serve my sentence, I will make amends by becoming a better, more mindful person, conscious of my responsibility to follow rules. By participating in self-directed learning programs, and those directed by my Unit Team, I intend to reenter the community as a law-abiding, productive citizen.

Through my research, I read an inspiring statement by Colette Peters, the new Director of the Bureau of Prisons. When testifying before the committee on the Judiciary on September 29, 2022, Director Peters said

> *"Our mission is to ensure safe prisons, humane correctional practices, and rehabilitation opportunities so that people reenter society as good neighbors."*

Up until the day that I learned of the investigation, I considered myself a good citizen. Once I began going through the criminal justice system, I realized how I failed my community, my profession, and my family.

I want to make things right.

Toward that end, I spent a lot of time working to prepare before sentencing. I had never been in trouble with the law before and I wanted to understand the goals of our judicial system. With time to plan, I studied websites that belong to the Department of Justice and the U.S. Courts. That research led me to learn the purpose of sentencing.

Federal judges impose sentences that should:

1. Deter other people from committing crimes,

2. Punish people for committing crimes,

3. Isolate people while they serve sentences, and

4. Rehabilitate people who commit crimes.

As a defendant, I did not have any way of influencing deterrence, punishment, or isolation. Those goals would serve the interest of justice, but my judge would impose the term that would accomplish such goals.

When it came to rehabilitation, however, I had to think. I realize that "rehabilitation" isn't only about me. It's about the entire system, the entire country. To reconcile with society, I would have to make the most of that term. Doing so would require me to find ways to live with meaning and relevance and usefulness.

I hope you will see beyond the surface of my current circumstances and consider the totality of my life. As a 42-year old college graduate, I deeply regret my actions and the consequences that they have entailed. But I humbly request you to consider the life I led before this unfortunate incident, and my unwavering commitment to service.

I accept the full weight of my actions, and affirm my deep remorse, acknowledging the pain and harm I have inflicted. I am aware of the wrongness of my deeds, and I carry the burden of guilt with a heavy heart.

As a follower of the Catholic faith, I have been taught that God gives each of us talents, gifts that we are encouraged to use for the betterment of those around us. The parable of the talents in the Bible has always moved me, reminding me of my obligation to use what God has given me for good. But I admit that I misused my talents, causing more harm than good. For this, I am truly sorry.

In my faith, there is also a strong emphasis on repentance and making amends. It is not enough to merely acknowledge wrongdoing, but one must also strive to rectify it. To this end, I fully accept the consequences of my actions, and I view my forthcoming time in prison not as a punishment, but as a time for reflection and amends. I see it as a path to redemption.

While incarcerated, I intend to do all in my power to make amends for my wrongdoings and seek ways to use my talents in a positive and lawful manner. I hope to contribute to the community within the prison and to society, to provide some measure of restitution for the harm I've caused.

I am keenly aware that my actions have broken trust and caused harm. It is my fervent hope and commitment to rebuild that trust, not through mere words, but through consistent actions that demonstrate my resolve to change.

I am resolved to turn my remorse into a meaningful change, to ensure that my future actions reflect the lessons I have learned from this painful experience.

The charge against me read: United States of America v. Your Name. For that reason, I feel a duty to make amends to every citizen in this country. While awaiting my surrender, I devised a plan to reconcile and atone. During my term, I intend to work toward that end, and I will continue living in service upon release.

With approval from my Unit Team, I hope to accomplish the following tasks:

» Tutor other people serving sentences so that they may advance their education.

» Volunteer in ways that staff members recommend.

» Journal about my progress and share those writings with our community.

» Read books that will help me become more aware of the influences that led me into this problem.

» Reflect on what I learn from reading, and then I will apply those lessons to volunteer work that I intend to complete upon my release.

I hope my Unit Team will support the personal release plan that I put into place and consider me a good candidate for maximum placement on home confinement, for reasons expressed below.

COMMUNITY SUPPORT:

To show community support, I offer the following letters for my unit team to consider. I intend to live at home with my wife and mother once my unit team and the Bureau of Prisons authorize. Our home is located at the following address:

18242 Bollinger Way
Wichita, KS 79852

Our home is in a quiet neighborhood, with low crime rates. My wife and I purchased this home more than ten years ago and it will be an ideal place for me to recalibrate. I will be able to work from home, and care for my aging mother. My wife and mother would live in the home with me.

The letters below show that I have their support.

Wife: Katherine Sample

My name is Katherine, and I am writing to express my unwavering support for my husband, Michael Sample, who was recently sentenced to serve a 30-month term in federal prison for securities fraud. While I fully acknowledge the gravity of his mistake, I want to emphasize that Michael is a man of integrity, and this isolated incident does not define the person I have known and loved for over two decades.

I have been married to Michael for the past 20 years, and during this time, I have come to know him as a compassionate, honest, and hardworking individual. Our journey began in college, where we met and discovered a shared passion for building a life of meaning and purpose together. Throughout our marriage, Michael has consistently demonstrated unwavering dedication to our family and his professional endeavors, always striving to uphold the values he holds dear.

It deeply saddens me to witness the consequences of his actions, which have not only affected us as a family but have also caused harm to others. I firmly believe that he deeply regrets his actions and is determined to learn from this experience, making amends wherever possible. I am confident that this unfortunate situation has the potential to be a turning point in his life, prompting him to become an even better and more responsible member of society.

Given the circumstances, I humbly request the Bureau of Prisons to exercise discretion and consider the possibility of allowing Michael to transfer to home confinement at the soonest appropriate time. Our family home is a place of love, support, and understanding, and I can assure you that we are fully prepared to welcome Michael and provide the necessary support for his reintegration into society.

The transition from prison to home confinement, under appropriate supervision, would enable Michael to continue serving his sentence while being in a more conducive environment for personal growth and rehabilitation. This would also allow him to contribute to our family's financial responsibilities and provide the op-

portunity to participate in rehabilitative programs that promote self-improvement and a deeper understanding of the consequences of his actions.

I understand the gravity of the offense, and I do not seek to downplay its seriousness. However, I firmly believe in the importance of second chances and the potential for redemption. With our family's support, Michael will have a strong foundation to rebuild his life and demonstrate his commitment to being a productive and law-abiding member of society.

Thank you for considering my request. Your discretion and careful evaluation of Michael's circumstances are greatly appreciated. If necessary, I am willing to provide any additional information or support documentation that may aid in this process.

Sincerely,
Katherine Sample
    Email: KatherineSample@gmail.com
    Cell: 423-xxx-xxxx

Mother: Angela Sample

I am writing this letter with a heavy heart to express my unwavering support for my son, Michael Sample, who has recently been sentenced to serve a 30-month term in federal prison for securities fraud. As a 77-year-old widow with health challenges, Michael has been my sole caregiver, providing the love, support, and assistance that I depend on daily.

I suffer from diabetes and am confined to a wheelchair, making everyday tasks a tremendous challenge for me. Michael has been my rock, dedicating himself to ensuring my well-being and happiness. He drives me to my medical appointments, assists with my medications, and tends to my needs with unfaltering care and devotion. His presence has been a source of strength, and without him, I fear my quality of life will greatly suffer.

I understand the severity of Michael's actions and the need for him to be held accountable for his mistakes. However, I implore the Bureau of Prisons to consider the unique circumstances of our situation. Home confinement could be a viable alternative to allow Michael to continue serving his sentence while still fulfilling his crucial role as my caregiver.

While I acknowledge that there may be conditions and restrictions to ensure he complies with the terms of his sentence, I believe that the comfort and familiarity of our family home would foster an environment where Michael can reflect on his actions and work towards rehabilitation effectively.

I assure you that our home is equipped to meet the requirements set forth by the Bureau of Prisons, and I am committed to assisting Michael in any way necessary to ensure compliance with his sentence. We understand the seriousness of his offense, and it is our intention to work together to rebuild trust and demonstrate his commitment to being a responsible and law-abiding member of society.

Taking Michael away from our home during this challenging time would not only have a profound emotional impact on both of us but would also place an immense burden on me, as I have no other immediate family to turn to for care and support.

I respectfully request that the Bureau of Prisons carefully considers our situation and grants Michael the opportunity for home confinement. This decision would not only alleviate the strain on our family but would also allow him to continue supporting me during my time of need.

Thank you for your understanding and consideration. I am willing to provide any additional information or documentation required to support our request.

Sincerely,
Angela Sample
    Email: AngelaSample@Gmail.com
    Cell: 423-xxx-xxxx

MEDICAL PRESCRIPTIONS AND SUBSTANCE ABUSE:

I am a 42-year-old male, standing at 5'9" and weighing 240 pounds. Diabetes has been a part of my life for some time now, and it is essential for me to manage this condition effectively to ensure my well-being.

To control my diabetes, my healthcare provider has prescribed the following medication:

Metformin: I take Metformin regularly as part of my treatment plan. This medication is crucial in improving my insulin sensitivity, helping my body regulate blood glucose levels more efficiently.

Managing my diabetes effectively is of utmost importance to me, as it allows me to lead a healthier life and minimize the risk of complications associated with the condition.

While I recognize the seriousness of the situation that led to my incarceration, I humbly request that the Bureau of Prisons consider the significance of proper diabetes management. Maintaining a consistent and stable routine for my medication, diet, and blood glucose monitoring is crucial to my overall health.

I also have a history of alcoholism, but I believe that I have that under control now. I know that I need to lose weight, and I will work on fitness during my imprisonment.

FINANCIAL OBLIGATIONS:

Besides sentencing me to serve a 30-month sentence, my judge imposed restitution in the amount of $435,671.98. I have $250,000 toward that fine. While incarcerated, I intend to comply with the Financial Responsibility Program. I have read about that program statement:

> » https://prisonprofessors.com/wp-content/uploads/2022/07/FRP-Plan-5380_008.pdf

I will do my best to comply with the requirements of that program.

RISK AND NEEDS ASSESSMENT:

From reading the Bureau of Prisons' website, I learned a great deal about risk and needs assessments.

> » https://www.bop.gov/inmates/fsa/docs/fsa_needs_assessment_overview.pdf

Once I surrender, it's my understanding that the Bureau of Prisons will require that I complete a SPARC-13 survey. My responses to the survey will help staff members measure 13 factors that can influence criminal behavior:

1. Anger/hostility: I am not an angry person.

2. Antisocial peers: I do not socialize or interact with people who violate the law.

3. Cognitions: I am a good learner.

4. Dyslexia: I do not suffer from dyslexia.

5. Education: I have several advanced degrees and I am a trained accountant.

6. Family/parenting: I have excellent relationships with my three children.

7. Finance/poverty: I am financially stable.

8. Medical: I am in excellent health.

9. Mental Health: I feel mentally strong.

10. Recreation/Leisure/Fitness: While I serve my sentence, I intend to stay fit by walking.

11. Substance abuse: I intend to participate in any available classes to treat my alcoholism.

12. Trauma: I grew up in a war torn country, and still feel trauma by some of the abuse I witnessed.

13. Work: I am a hard worker and will continue to work to the best of my ability.

PERSONAL PLAN:

While serving my sentence, I will follow the guidance of my Unit Team. Before surrendering, I began to volunteer with a nonprofit organization that works to improve outcomes for people serving sentences in the Bureau of Prisons. I discovered the group from a link on the BOP's website. The group focuses on helping people in prison prepare for success upon release.

Given the reality of my sentence, I began inquiring about ways that I could help. I worked together with the nonprofit to create coursework that would teach people how they can develop self-directed learning resources and build effective release plans. Those plans should help individuals overcome the challenges of a criminal conviction and live as a law-abiding, contributing citizens. Working through these lessons will help me stay productive while I serve my sentence.

While incarcerated, I intend to devote my time to creating more lesson plans that the nonprofit can use to expand. I will participate in one of the exercises, that includes reading intentionally, and to the extent possible, to teaching strategies that others can use to reach their highest potential, even while living in adversity.

On the Bureau of Prisons' website, I found Program Statement 5350.27: Inmate Manuscripts. It complies with the Code of Federal Regulations, which holds that:

"An inmate may prepare a manuscript for private use or for publication while in custody without staff approval."

The above Program Statement encourages me, as I intend to comply with all rules. To the extent possible, I intend to write about lessons I've learned about community service and contribution.

I plan to read several books while in prison. Prior to surrendering, I developed a reading list to help me grow as a person. I hope to learn lessons that will give me the tools necessary to avoid transgressing the laws of the United States or any of the rights of people which those laws were enacted to protect. I set a goal of writing a book report for each book that I read. Those book reports will detail:

» Why I chose to read the book.

» What I learned from reading the book.

» How reading the book will contribute to my success upon release.

I have organized my reading list into the six sections set forth below. I designed those sections in response to what I've read about risk assessments and the SPARC-13.

Thought – Books on personal growth will help me become a more thoughtful person and better member of the broader community. Books on thought would address the SPARC-13's emphasis on cognitions.

Finance – I have been working in the financial industry for longer than 14 years and I have learned a lot. There is always room to learn and grow. I would like to develop my understanding of how to manage financial affairs properly and efficiently better than what I currently know. Books on finance would address the SPARC-13's emphasis on finance/poverty.

Business / Marketing / Sales – Given the SPARC-13's emphasis on work, I thought it would be helpful to read books that would contribute to the career that I want to build upon release.

Biography: Given the SPARC-13's emphasis on mental health, I have selected a series of biographies so that I can learn from people who've lived as contributing citizens. This book should address criminogenic needs of antisocial peers, education, and mental health.

While serving my sentence, I would like to tutor, teach, and offer guidance in any way the Unit Team deems appropriate. Through these community-building efforts, I hope to work toward improving the culture that confines me.

Besides adhering to my own plan, I also will follow guidance from the experts in the BOP.

ADVISORS:

I have collaborated with my wife and mother in developing this release plan. They will be my accountability partners and help me stay true to the plan. I will continue to evolve the plan as I receive guidance from my unit team.

» Staff Guides: Federal Prison:

» Unit Manager Name:

» Case Manager Name: Counselor Name:

» Work Detail Supervisor:

» Halfway house Supervisor:

» Probation Officer:

SUPPLEMENTAL PROMPTS

EVOLVE YOUR RELEASE PLAN:

Consider your release plan in stages. If you were to address "all" aspects of your release plan today, you would not have a good plan. The plan must grow. Presumably, as calendar pages turn, you will celebrate a series of incremental achievements. You will leverage those achievements to put yourself on the pathway to new opportunities. Through this deliberate process, you will restore confidence and create new opportunities. Those opportunities will advance your prospects for success upon release. They will help you advocate when you encounter challenges that afflict most all justice-impacted people.

You must plan for a successful return to society. That plan must evolve, maturing over time. To the extent that you can point to your plan and show how your success resulted from your plan, and how you adjusted as you encountered changes, you can show that you're the CEO of your life. You will restore confidence, and you will convert adversaries into advocates, opening new opportunities along the way.

PRISON PROFESSORS TALENT:

With that end in mind, we created Prison Professors Talent. It is a website that will allow you to memorialize your journey. It's never too early, and it's never too late to begin showing that you created a plan to work toward success—as you define success.

As stated earlier, anyone can begin a profile by adhering to the steps we detailed earlier in this workbook. To recap:

Step 1:

» Send an email to <u>Interns@PrisonProfessorsTalent.com</u>

» Prison Professors Charitable Corporation

32565 Golden Lantern Street, B-1026
Dana Point, CA 92629

Step 2:

» Write a biography to help your audience know you better. You will evolve this biography over time.

Step 3:

» Write a journal to describe how you're working to prepare for your success upon release.

Step 4:

» Write book reports to document what you're learning.

Step 5:

» Publish your release plan, or at least the parts that you want to share.

Then, develop your profile by adding to it regularly. It will become an asset that you use to overcome the challenges ahead.

Below we offer some prompts that you may consider adding to your profile, through your journal page or other areas as you evolve.

Prompts to Develop your Profile and Release Plan

MISSION STATEMENT:

Consider writing a personal mission statement. It's something that the Bureau of Prisons will recognize. For example, Collette Peters, the Director of the BOP, published the following:

Mission:

» Corrections professionals who foster a humane and secure environment and ensure public safety by preparing individuals for successful reentry into our communities.

Vision: Proposed future state for the BOP

» Our highly skilled diverse and innovate workforce creates a strong foundation of safety and security, through the principles of humanity and normalcy we develop good neighbors.

CORE Values:

» Accountability: We are responsible and transparent to the public, ourselves, and to those in our care and custody, by the standards we establish, the actions we take, and the duties we perform.

Integrity:

» We are true to our ethical standards in all circumstances.

Respect:

» We foster an inclusive environment where the viewpoints of employees, the public, and those in our care and custody are considered and valued.

Compassion:

» We will strive to understand one another's circumstances and act with empathy and by we, we mean each other as colleagues and corrections professionals and compassion for those in our care and custody.

Correctional Excellence.

» We demonstrate leadership in our corrections field through our practices and values.

Consider how you could follow this example, giving credit to the system.

GOALS:

What goals would you like to accomplish as you engineer your release plan, at various stages:

» 12 months

» 36 months

» 60 months

» 120 months

EDUCATION/VOCATION:

What education and training goals did you set and accomplish during your imprisonment?

» How will your education or training influence your success?

» In what ways do you anticipate developing your career?

» In what ways are you training to develop your career?

» In what ways are you developing your curriculum vitae?

» What challenges or barriers do you anticipate in the employment market?

» In what ways does your release plan address those barriers?

FINANCE / INCOME / EXPENSES:

» Describe the financial balance sheet that you anticipate upon release:

» What do you anticipate in the ways of capital needs to establish your life upon release?

» What financial obligations will you encounter upon release?

» In what ways are you preparing to meet those financial obligations?

FIRST 90 DAYS:

» What level of liquidity do you anticipate on the day of your release?

» What projections do you have for expenses during the first 90 days of your liberty?

» How would you describe your budget during the first 90 days of your liberty?

» What level of liquidity do you anticipate 90 days after your release?

» How will you track your budget?

» What strategies have you devised to build supplemental income streams?

SOCIAL SUPPORT:

» Describe the mentors who have advised you since you began serving your sentence.

» In what ways have you worked to improve your support group during your journey?

» How would you describe your board of advisors?

» In what ways will they advise you?

» What responsibilities will you have with parenting?

» In what ways have you prepared for parening?

COLLATERAL CONSEQUENCES:

» In what ways have you addressed the mental-health challenges that come with being a justice-impacted person?

» How have the strategies you've engineered contributed to your success upon release?

» What tools, tactics, and resources have you built to address the collateral consequences of being a justice-impacted person?

» What obstacles do you anticipate facing because of your conviction?

» In what ways have you prepared to address those obstacles?

HOW TO WRITE A BIO

A compelling profile on Prison Professors Talent should begin with a biography.

Those who've gone through our course, Preparing for Success after Prison, know that Frederick Douglass inspired me to think about bios at the start of my sentence. His life story shows us the power of memorializing a life story.

Although born into slavery, Frederick Douglass wrote three biographies. He used those biographies as practical tools that would advance his life. Over time, Mr. Douglass became one of the world's most influential advocates, leading to the abolition of slavery.

If a person wants to overcome a crisis, or contribute to solutions, the person must help others understand the motivations behind the decision. That biography should evolve over time.

REPUTATION:

Regardless of what goals a person wants to pursue after prison, each person should consider the power of the internet. People frequently scour the internet before they make decisions.

- » Before hiring a person, employers frequently use the internet to learn what they can find about a person's background.

- » Before doing business, people look online to see what they can understand about a person.

- » Before purchasing a product or service, a person may research people with whom they're about to do business.

- » Before extending credit, lenders will use the internet to learn what they can.

People who want to prepare for success after prison should think about those challenges. Building a public record helped me immensely, and it's one of the reasons that I recommend others take the time to write a biography.

Although I served 26 years in prison for a greatest-severity drug offense, my criminal background does not block me from opportunities. Nor does the criminal record define my life. Rather, the biography shows resilience, and resilience inspires confidence.

People do business with me because they can see the methodical, systematic steps I took to prepare for success after prison. Building trust begins by telling our story.

When writing a biography for an online profile, consider the audience. That audience may include the following people:

» Administrators in prison who have discretion over release dates,

» Probation officers that may decide how much liberty to grant,

» Employers that consider offering income opportunities,

» Lenders who may extend capital, and

» Anyone who wants to open a relationship.

When searching online, those people will likely see government press releases. If a person takes time to write a biography, people will see how hard a person has worked to make amends and reconcile with society. A good profile will give people a different perspective, shaping new opportunities.

EXAMPLE OF A BIO:

As an example, people can view the biography I wrote under my profile. It shows the entire journey, with many links that anyone can easily follow. Those links show authenticity. They show the methodical steps I took to prepare for success upon release. By writing that biography, many opportunities opened—as anyone can read about in my book Earning Freedom: Conquering a 45-Year Prison Term, or by going through our course, Preparing for Success after Prison.

The stories of Frederick Douglass, Nelson Mandela, Viktor Frankl, Mahatma Gandhi, and others inspired me. They showed me how to use time in prison to prepare for a life of meaning, relevance, and dignity upon release. If participants write their biographies, they will go a long way toward showing their resilience. By showing resilience, opportunities open.

Below I offer some tips for writing a compelling biography:

INTROSPECT:

Write about all you've learned by going through this experience. Show that you've developed a deeper understanding of all your previous decisions that led to where you are today.

SELF-AWARENESS:

Show that you have a clear understanding of your strengths, weaknesses, opportunities, and threats. Demonstrate that you don't make excuses but set goals and pursue success.

RESILIENCE:

Shape your narrative by focusing on the plan that you've made to overcome and triumph over a criminal background. We're all human beings, and we all fall. When we have the strength to stand up and own our past, we begin to carve a brighter future.

GOAL-SETTING AND PLANNING:

Describe what you're striving to achieve and show the systematic steps you're taking to advance your life. By showing that you know how to work through challenges and prepare for success, you open more opportunities for people to support you.

ITERATIVE:

Develop your biography over time. It should become an integral part of your release plan. Use your bio to show that you're becoming more valuable over time and show your hard work on personal development.

SAMPLE BIO:

The information below is a sample bio. We encourage you to write a document that helps readers understand who you are at this phase of your life. Show that you're on a pathway to making better decisions in the future. You should write new versions of the bio as you progress through the journey to show your commitment to preparing for success.

At the age of 20, I made a regrettable decision to sell cocaine. Authorities arrested me when I was 23. A jury convicted me, and a judge sentenced me to serve 45 years in prison. Early in my sentence, I made a commitment to reconcile with society and work toward building credentials that would empower me to live as a law-abiding, contributing citizen.

I created a detailed release plan that carried me through 9,500 days in prison. That release plan would allow me to return to society strong, with my dignity intact and opportunities to prosper. I've built a career around that journey, advocating for reforms that I believed would improve outcomes for all justice-impacted people. The biography, and the validating links below, show that I never ask anyone to do anything that I did not do to work toward the best possible outcome.

None of us can change the past, but we can all work to make amends and create a better future. Justice-impacted people should engineer an effective release plan, use that plan to build a better future, and memorialize the measurable, incremental progress they make.

All the courses I create provide guidance on how to prepare for success upon release:

>> Step 1: Start by defining success as the best possible outcome,

>> Step 2: Create a release plan that will lead from crisis to prosperity,

>> Step 3: Set priorities, to accomplish first things first,

>> Step 4: Build tools, tactics, and resources that will advance the plan,

>> Step 5: Create accountability tools to measure progress,

>> Step 6: Open supportive networks and relationships, and

>> Step 7: Adjust the plan as necessary, but execute the plan every day.

I used those seven steps above to prepare for success upon release from prison. I strive to teach others how to navigate the crisis of a criminal conviction and work toward building lives of meaning, contribution, and relevance.

BACKSTORY:

Since the crime of leading an enterprise that sold cocaine carried a potentially lengthy sentence, administrators in the detention center locked me in solitary confinement. In the beginning, all I wanted was to get out of prison. Misguided, I proceeded through a trial despite being guilty of the crime.

The jury convicted me of all counts.

Following the conviction, a kind officer in the detention center brought me books. Those biographies introduced me to the transformative stories of Frederick Douglass, Nelson Mandela, Socrates, and Viktor Frankl. Inspired by these figures, I crafted a three-pronged release plan to guide me through prison. I would focus on the following:

» Educating myself,

» Contributing to society, and

» Building a positive support network.

Rather than allow the sentence or prison walls to define me, I used all my time inside to prepare for success upon release.

Through that commitment, I earned a bachelor's and a master's degree during my imprisonment. Then I authored books. Those books helped me to build a solid and influential support network. I even married the love of my life during my 16th year of confinement, and we've built a life together.

TEACHING AND ADVOCACY

Upon my release, San Francisco State University hired me to work as an adjunct professor. I created a unique course, "The Architecture of Incarceration," to foster a deeper understanding of prison systems and how we could improve them by incentivizing excellence among prisoners. I used my book, "Earning Freedom,"

to illustrate my vision for a system where prisoners could work toward earning their freedom.

The release plan that led me through prison opened opportunities for me to begin advocating for reforms that would incentivize a pursuit of excellence. Anyone can read the historical efforts that began early in my journey:

Seattle Times, 2006

Forbes Magazine, 2008

Stanford Law School, 2012

Robina Institute, 2016

Teaching and advocacy require a long-term commitment. A plan keeps a person on course, even in the face of adversity.

PRISON PROFESSORS: A BEACON OF HOPE

Following my belief in the power of rehabilitation, I founded Prison Professors. I designed courses that would prepare individuals in prison for a successful life upon release. Over 300,000 people have accessed our flagship course, "Preparing for Success after Prison," which helps participants define success, set clear goals, and cultivate attitudes and behaviors conducive to personal and professional development.

IMPACTFUL SUCCESS STORIES

I am particularly proud of our success stories, especially Halim Flowers's. Halim was serving a double life sentence. Halim managed to secure his release through his commitment to preparing for success upon release and has since flourished as a successful artist and activist.

ADVOCACY AND FUTURE GOALS

I began advocating for incentives decades ago, as shown through my published writings, my work as a professor, and my work helping influential people

understand the importance of incentivizing excellence. You can see the history of that advocacy with the following links:

Inside: Life Behind Bars in America, 2006

» St. Martin's Press published this book that I wrote as I approached my 20th year of imprisonment. The book would teach readers about the system, and build a case for legislative changes that would empower staff members to incentivize people to work toward gradual increases in liberty.

Earning Freedom, 2012

» As I worked through my final year in prison, I wrote Earning Freedom. I intended to use this book to build a career around all I learned while growing through 26 years in prison and to advocate for reforms that would bring more incentives into the system.

San Francisco Chronicle, 2012

» The release plan that guided me through 8,500 days in prison opened many opportunities. By memorializing my journey, other influential people learned how hard I worked to prepare for success upon release. The editor of the San Francisco Chronicle reached out to inquire about writing an interview.

San Francisco State University, 2012

» As a result of a front-page story that the San Francisco Chronicle published upon my release, San Francisco State University offered me a position to teach as an adjunct professor. In that role, I could help criminal justice students learn why incentives would increase productivity and lower recidivism rates in our nation's criminal justice system.

UC Berkeley, 2012

» When Dr. Alan Ross, at UC Berkeley, learned of the release plan that guided me through prison, and the advocacy work I was doing to improve outcomes, he invited me to make a presentation at UC Berkeley. I hired a videographer to memorialize the event.

Stanford University Law School, 2013

» While I served my sentence, many mentors came into my life. Joan Petersilia, for example, of Stanford Law School, invited me to publish a chapter for her scholarly book: The Oxford Handbook of Sentencing and Corrections. I contributed a chapter to her book, arguing for the need of incentives. Professor Robert Weisberg, Co-Director of the Stanford Criminal Justice Center published the following testimonial in his commencement speech to the Stanford Law, on June 15, 2013:

> *"Closer to home, a few months ago some of our students met Michael Santos. Michael is one of our leading commentators on sentencing and correctional policy in the U.S. He has written great scholarly articles on criminal justice and will play a major role in criminal law reform in the coming years. But Michael invented his self by an act of arduous, muscular imagination when, at the age of 23, he was sitting in a federal prison for drug crimes he has never denied. He imagined a self that he could be at the end of a certain 25 years of federal incarceration, and it was only because he had that new self in mind that he could persevere through the self-education and character rebuilding that made him what he is.*

Robert Weisberg, Stanford Law Graduation, June 15, 2013, Page 4

UC Hastings Law School, 2015

» The law school at UC Hastings invited me to make a presentation at a symposium for changes to sentencing laws. The presentation included an article in the UC Hastings Law Review, titled Incentivizing Excellence.

Ninth Circuit Correctional Summit, 2015

» Through my work at Stanford, UC Berkeley, SFSU, and UC Hastings Law School, I got to interact with many members of law enforcement, including US Attorneys and federal judges. Judges from the Ninth Circuit Court of Appeals invited me to keynote a presentation at a correctional summit.

Department of Justice, 2016

» Our work with federal judges led to work with the Department of Justice, including an invitation to visit Guam and Saipan to introduce our course,

Preparing for Success after Prison, to the correctional system in Micronesia.

<u>Bureau of Prisons, 2017</u>

» We began working with the Federal Bureau of Prisons at USP Atwater, then FCC Florence. After successful implementation of our program, Preparing for Success after Prison in high-security penitentiaries, we broadened our relationship. We now offer our course in every federal prison in the North Central Region,

<u>California Department of Corrections, 2017</u>

» We now work in every state prison in the state of California, and thousands of people earn milestone credits when the complete Preparing for Success after Prison.

The signing of the First Step Act in 2018 marked a significant victory. This law enables individuals to earn higher levels of liberty through merit and preparations for success. I continue to fight for further reforms to reduce recidivism rates and empower incarcerated individuals to transition successfully into society.

We're working to improve outcomes for all justice-impacted people through Prison Professors. We can build safer communities by teaching hundreds of thousands of people how to create effective release plans. Through the data we collect, we hope to influence legislation that further incentivizes prisoners to work toward earning increased levels of liberty.

Some of those advocacy efforts include:

» Work release programs for people in federal prison,

» Expanded access to compassionate release,

» Meaningful access to clemency,

» Furloughs for people who qualify,

» Reinstatement of US Parole

PERSONAL LIFE

Despite the challenging circumstances, I built a fulfilling personal life during my incarceration. I married Carole Santos during my 16th year of imprisonment in 2003. We nurtured our marriage during my final decade in prison. Revenues generated by my work in prison allowed Carole to return to school and become a master's educated registered nurse. She now works closely with me as an integral partner in our shared mission to improve the outcomes of America's prison system.

Besides working on our family businesses, Carole and I enjoy working on our investment projects that bring value to society.

A MESSAGE OF HOPE

I want my journey to serve as a reminder that regardless of past mistakes, everyone can work toward becoming a better version of themselves. We, as a society, should create mechanisms to encourage this progress.

A JOURNEY OF RESILIENCE

Thanks to leaders like Frederick Douglass, Socrates, Nelson Mandela, and others, I learned the power of resilience. Any of us can transform our lives, despite past mistakes.

HOW TO JOURNAL

To build an amazing profile that inspires others, a person should show daily progress. For that reason, Prison Professors Talent opens an opportunity to document the ways that participants use time in prison to prepare for success upon release.

As an example, I published a series of journal entries to show how journals helped me prepare for success while I went through 9,500 days in prison. The journals continue to be an integral component for my ongoing preparations for success.

People may want to consider journaling as a tactic for self-advocacy.

JUDGES AND JOURNALING:

Federal judges sentence people to the custody of the attorney general. They consider the information put before them by prosecutors, defense attorneys, and probation officers. They do not have any way of knowing what the person will do in the months, years, or decades ahead.

Many leaders advise that people should always think about the best possible outcome. If people know what they want, they can engineer a pathway more likely to succeed.

People in prison want opportunities to advance release dates and have a higher level of liberty as soon as possible.

If an opportunity opens for resentencing, or if laws and policies open more opportunities to incentivize excellence, the person should have resources that will help people with discretion understand the work that went into preparing for success. A daily journal can document the record.

At the start of every year, I wrote specific goals I wanted to achieve. Those goals aligned with how I defined success. For example:

I wrote how many books I intended to read during the year,

» I wrote how many miles I would run during the year,

» I wrote how many courses I would complete during the year,

» I wrote the number of books I pledged to read during the year.

» I documented the reason behind all those decisions.

Daily journals memorialized how I used time in prison to prepare for success upon release. Those records opened new opportunities that led to income opportunities, early termination of Supervised Release, and liberty to launch advocacy efforts.

I concluded my obligation to the Bureau of Prisons in August, 2013. Since then, I've continued to document my path. The journals open opportunities. We grow stronger when we show our resilience, and journals can help.

As human beings, we all face challenges and crises. Resilience requires us to:

» Launch plans to overcome,

» Prioritize the steps we must take,

» Build our tools, tactics, and resources,

» Measure our progress with daily accountability, adjusting as necessary,

» Execute our plan every day.

Daily journals help us stay on track with the plans we set. For that reason, I continue to journal about the methodical steps I'm taking to work toward my goals. All those goals relate to success, as I define success.

If you're working through our course, Preparing for Success after Prison, try to memorialize your journey. Writing a journal entry regularly helped me through prison, and the strategy continues to help me open opportunities.

Consider writing a journal each day. Make the journal transparent, and you will take a huge step toward building a support network that wants to invest in you. If an opportunity opens for you to appear before a judge, or to influence people with discretion to ease your life, the daily journal will become an invaluable asset. It will show how hard you worked to prepare for success upon release, and that is a self-advocacy technique that will serve you well.

Consider the following question:

> » In what ways would a daily journal from yesterday show your preparation for higher levels of success?

Our community at PrisonProfessorsTalent.com opens opportunities to memorialize your preparations.

SAMPLE JOURNAL ENTRY

The information below is a sample journal entry. Please visit my profile on Prison Professors Talent to see more samples. I would use these samples as a resource to persuade others of my commitment to preparing for success. It helped stakeholders see me differently.

People who journal regularly put themselves on a pathway of resilience.

Journals open opportunities to collaborate. In today's entry, I'll offer insight that I hope our community can use.

Journaling opened opportunities that empowered me while I served my sentence.

They allowed me to build relationships that helped me overcome complications.

Once I got out, the journals influenced my liberty and income.

As a critical-thinking exercise, readers may want to venture a guess as to how. Or, they can read today's journal to learn more.

OPENING OPPORTUNITIES:

Those who read Earning Freedom may recall that I devised a plan to guide me through my first decade in prison. By the time I served ten years, I wanted:

> » To earn a university degree,
>
> » Publish at least one article, chapter, or book, and
>
> » Ten people who would advocate on my behalf.

Those three prongs became a compass for me. I would consult my compass when taking a step or making a choice. Every decision came with an opportunity cost, and I always tried to work toward what I thought would help me prepare for success upon release.

Since I knew what I wanted within ten years, I could reverse engineer the progress I should make. The daily journals became my accountability metrics. I could see whether I was on track and making progress or whether I needed to adjust my activities.

In December, I set goals I wanted to achieve the following year. The daily journals would keep me on track. I'd write a quarterly report at the end of March, June, and September. At the end of the year, I'd write an annual report.

I learned that strategy by watching CNBC. Business leaders devised accountability tools to help them measure progress. Their progress helped them stay on track and create value. My daily journals would help me do the same thing. They empowered me. Instead of dwelling over how I would get through ten years (or a 45-year sentence), I grew stronger by seeing the progress I could make each day.

BUILDING RELATIONSHIPS:

I built credibility by documenting the daily progress and showing how each step related to a greater goal. The journal became a tool or a tactic. I could use the journal to persuade others to see me differently. Although I could not change my conviction or sentence length, I could influence how others perceived me. Since I didn't want my criminal conviction to define my life, I devised the journaling strategy to show how I could master and grow through crisis.

When I encountered people I wanted to bring into my network, I could show them copies of my daily journal, quarterly reports, or annual report. Those resources became an opportunity to reframe perceptions. People like Professor Joan Petersilia of Stanford Law School invited me to publish with her. Had I not written the daily journals or shared my reports with her, I would not have developed that relationship while I served my sentence.

A relationship with a distinguished professor from Stanford Law School helped me overcome many complications. It also helped me to open relationships with other influential people.

LIBERTY AND INCOME:

As a result of the journals, San Francisco's major newspaper, The Chronicle, showed an interest in me when I got out. The editor reached out and asked if the newspaper could profile my story. People in San Francisco, he said, would find interest in what it was like to return to society after multiple decades in prison.

Had it not been for the daily journals, the editor of a major newspaper would not have known me. Had he not known me, the newspaper would not have published a story about how I prepared for success after prison on the front page.

Because of that front-page article in a major newspaper, many more opportunities opened. It influenced San Francisco State University to invite me to become a professor, it opened opportunities for me to invest in real estate, and it helped my probation officer to grant me a high level of liberty—including the ability to travel domestically without permission, the ability to work as an entrepreneur, and the ability to advocate for reforms and work with other justice-impacted people.

Journaling helped me prepare for success upon release. It's the reason I continue journaling today. To create opportunities out of nothing, we must show how our success results from daily commitment.

> » In what ways are you memorializing your daily commitment to a pursuit of excellence?

HOW TO WRITE BOOK REPORTS

To build a supportive network while serving time in prison, we must memorialize the investment we're making to prepare for success upon release. The sooner we start, the better off we are. Book reports can become a great tactic as part of a self-directed strategy to prepare for success.

HOW BOOK REPORTS HELPED ME CONQUER A 45-YEAR SENTENCE:

Several years into my sentence, I remember lying on the rack in my cell. I felt so grateful that I could read. I was alone, with decades remaining to serve. I felt thankful that I could see. Without vision, I wouldn't be able to read. And if I couldn't read, my time inside would challenge me. I wouldn't feel productive if I couldn't engineer ways to make my time count.

By reading, we can make our time count. We simply had to figure out how to read deliberately.

While staring at the ceiling and trying to sleep, I didn't count sheep. Instead, I tried to recall all the books I had read since DEA agents arrested me.

More than 35 years have passed since my arrest in 1987, but I still remember the first book I read in prison: The Flight of the Falcon. Before my arrest, I watched The Falcon and the Snowman, an espionage film with Sean Penn and Timothy Hutton. The film described two adolescents from good families who got into trouble. They broke the law and went to prison. In The Flight of the Falcon, I learned that one of the characters escaped.

In that solitary cell, I realized I had a choice. I could read books that would entertain me, or I could read books that would contribute to my preparation for success. Either option would help.

By reading well, I would learn how to structure language in ways that would make me a better communicator. Yet while trying to sleep and counting the books, I realized that I didn't remember all the books I had read since I began serving my sentence.

PROJECTING SUCCESS AFTER PRISON:

I started to project all the years that I would serve. By reading at least 50 books each year, I would read 500 in ten years. I could learn a lot. But if I had a record of each book I read, I believe I would have an asset that would open opportunities.

That idea prompted me to write book reports. Those book reports would memorialize the books I read. With hundreds of book reports, I'd have a record that I could use to open new opportunities.

The idea that began in that jail cell evolved into a template. Each time I read a book, I would write the author's name, the date I read the book, and then offer a response to three simple questions:

» Why I chose to read the book,

» What I learned from reading the book, and

» How the book would contribute to my success upon release.

That tactic became a part of my long-term strategy of preparing for success upon release. People viewed me differently when I showed the record of my accomplishments in prison. They opened opportunities for me. My detailed descriptions that showed how I used time in prison to prepare for success persuaded my case manager in the halfway house and my probation officer to grant me a higher level of liberty.

» In what ways are you using your time today to prepare for success in the months, years, and decades ahead?

Book Title:
» The Seven Habits of Highly Effective People

Book Author:
» Dr. Stephen Covey

Date Read:
» I read The Seven Habits of Highly Effective People early during my prison term.

Why I read:

» *The Seven Habits of Highly Effective People*:

A friend of mine sent me a letter about reading Stephen Covey's book on personal development. Since he knew of my commitment to work toward becoming a better version of myself, he recommended that I read the book. I ordered the book from the prison's library program.

What I learned from reading

» *The Seven Habits of Highly Effective People*:

In reading The 7 Habits of Highly Effective People, by Stephen Covey, I learned many lessons that would help me use time in prison to prepare for success upon release. Covey presents a holistic approach to personal and professional success, emphasizing principles that promote integrity, effectiveness, and self-mastery. I will share my key learnings and how they impacted my perspective.

Summary:

Covey's book revolves around the central idea that personal change and growth are the foundations of success. He introduces seven habits that, when practiced consistently, can transform individuals into highly effective people. The author emphasizes an inside-out approach, where character development precedes quick-fix solutions. By nurturing inner qualities, I have discovered the ability to create a lasting impact in both my personal and professional spheres.

Habit 1: Be Proactive:

The first habit taught me the importance of taking responsibility for my life and actions. I learned to exercise self-awareness, make conscious choices, and align my actions with my personal values. By being proactive, I have gained the power to shape my circumstances, transcend limitations, and respond effectively to challenges.

Habit 2: Begin with the End in Mind:

This habit has instilled in me the significance of having a clear vision and setting meaningful goals. I now understand the importance of envisioning the desired outcome before embarking on any endeavor. By aligning my

actions with long-term goals, I have gained a sense of purpose and direction in my life.

Habit 3: Put First Things First:

The third habit has empowered me to manage my time effectively and prioritize tasks. I have learned to discern between urgent and important matters using Covey's time management matrix. By focusing on important tasks rather than being driven solely by urgency, I have achieved a better balance between my personal and professional obligations.

Habit 4: Think Win-Win:

Covey's fourth habit taught me the power of collaboration and cooperation. I now embrace a mindset that seeks mutual benefits in all interactions. By fostering win-win relationships, I build trust and establish long-term partnerships. This shift from scarcity to abundance mentality has allowed me to nurture a culture of shared success.

Habit 5: Seek First to Understand, Then to be Understood:

The fifth habit has revolutionized my approach to communication. I now prioritize understanding others before expressing my own opinions. By practicing empathetic listening, I have fostered genuine connections, resolved conflicts, and built trust. This habit has helped me cultivate stronger relationships with others.

Habit 6: Synergize:

Covey's concept of synergy has transformed my perspective on collaboration. I now value and leverage diverse perspectives, fostering an environment where the whole is greater than the sum of its parts. By embracing collective creativity and encouraging collaboration, I have witnessed the emergence of innovative solutions and achieved results beyond individual efforts.

Habit 7: Sharpen the Saw:

The final habit has taught me the importance of continuous self-renewal and growth. I now prioritize my physical, mental, emotional, and spiritual well-being. By investing in self-care, lifelong learning, and aligning my ac-

tions with my personal values, I sustain my effectiveness and create a positive impact on others.

Conclusion:

Anyone can learn from reading The 7 Habits of Highly Effective People. I began using this resource to teach others in prison how they can use time inside to prepare for success outside.

How will reading The Seven Habits of Highly Effective People contribute to my preparations for success upon release?

I will use the lessons from Stephen Covey's book in my work. They will help me develop a framework to teach others. Although I'll give credit to what I learned from Stephen Covey, particularly his guidance of "seeking first to understand before being understood" to help others understand the importance of developing release plans to guide them from adversity to prosperity.

HOW TO EVOLVE THE RELEASE PLAN

When creating a profile on Prison Professors Talent, a person should begin by writing the following four sections:

Biography: This section helps readers understand more about the backstory and how a person defines success going forward.

Journal: This section should show a person's commitment to success, highlighting the daily progress toward specific goals detailed in the biography.

Book Reports: This section shows that a person invests energy and resources to learn in a self-directed way, regardless of what challenges exist in prison.

Release Plan: This section helps readers understand that the person's success isn't luck but the execution of a plan that the person engineered to prepare for success after release.

Tribe: This section should show how you're working to contribute to your community, helping more people prepare for success after prison.

Ideally, the person should create a release plan early—preferably before going to prison. But as we say through all our courses, it's never too early, and it's never too late to begin sowing seeds for a better outcome.

LEARNING TO CREATE A RELEASE PLAN:

I didn't know how to create a release plan when authorities charged me with violating crimes that would eventually lead to my serving 9,500 days in prison. When the agents took me into custody, I only thought about getting out. Despite knowing I had committed the crimes, I clung to a fantasy that my lawyer would persuade a jury to acquit me.

Without a plan, I didn't consider my strengths, weaknesses, opportunities, or threats. Instead of putting trust in a plan I could have created to navigate my way to a life of meaning, relevance, and dignity, I made decisions that exacerbated my problems.

After the jury convicted me, I became receptive to reading books that an officer brought to me in the Special Housing Unit. While locked alone in my cell, I read about people who transformed their life while in prison. They returned to society to lead productive lives when they finished their term.

I needed a plan that would help me turn my time inside into a better life. That goal required me to:

» Define the best possible outcome.

» Create a plan to help me cross the chasm from being in a prison cell to leaving prison successfully.

» Prioritize the first steps I would have to take to implement my plan.

» Develop tools, tactics, and resources that would accelerate my plan.

» Create tools to measure progress and hold myself accountable.,

» Adjust the plan as necessary.

» Execute the plan every day.

ITERATIVE RELEASE PLANS:

A good plan could help me restore confidence. It could show that I understood the gravity of my situation and help others see that I wanted to reconcile with society. Each step would lead me closer to the life I wanted once I finished serving my sentence.

I started making that plan after my conviction. The judge hadn't sentenced me yet, though the mandatory-minimum sentencing law required him to impose a lengthy term. My plan would focus on the first ten years. It would require that I work to:

» Earn academic credentials and get an education,

» Contribute to society in meaningful, measurable ways, and

» Build a strong support network that would help me advocate for better opportunities.

Since I understood that I would have to serve at least ten years, I needed that interim plan. It would carry me through time in a high-security penitentiary and later when I hoped to transfer to a medium-security prison.

DELIBERATE RELEASE PLANS:

Each person should create a deliberate plan that relates to his or her circumstances. A plan for a person with a multi-decade sentence would obviously differ from a person with an 18-month sentence. Define success, and make the plan. All plans, however, should cover the basics:

» What influences led you to prison?

» What do you understand about the reason why you're in prison?

» In what ways did the crime or conviction influence others in society?

» In what ways does your plan show that you're working to make amends?

» How are you holding yourself accountable?

» What challenges will you face in reaching the outcome you want?

» What strategies have you created to triumph over adversity?

» What level of progress should people expect from you?

» What tools, tactics, and resources can you create to advance your plan?

» What adjustments have you made to your plan since you began?

» The more thought you give to crafting your plan, the stronger you become.

The plan I created helped me grow through 26 years in federal prison, leading to a series of successful ventures when I returned to society. When obstacles or challenges surfaced, I adjusted my plans. This strategy carried me through prison and I continue to follow it today.

WHAT IS YOUR PLAN?

Our community at PrisonProfessorsTalent.com opens opportunities to memorialize your preparations. If you'd like to publish your profile, email our team:

Interns@PrisonProfessorsTalent.com.

Prison Professors Charitable Corporation
32565 Golden Lantern Street, B-1019
Dana Point, CA 92629

HOW TO BUILD A TRIBE

As human beings, we all face crises and one time or another. We can differentiate ourselves by showing how we respond. Some people ignore the problems or live in denial. Others plan a strategy to help them recalibrate, rebuild, and succeed.

Through our work at Prison Professors, we strive to show justice-impacted people how to respond after an arrest or criminal prosecution. They've got to create a plan. The plan should address specific challenges and different stages. Ultimately, the plan should help people recalibrate so they can go on to live with meaning and relevance, and dignity.

They may accelerate the plan if they work to restore and rebuild a reputation.

We're in the digital age, which makes it easy for people to learn about a person's criminal record. If not appropriately addressed, that record can complicate a person's pathway to success. Even after a person serves a prison term, collateral consequences await. We must prepare.

While it may seem like an uphill battle, a well-executed personal marketing strategy can significantly impact public perception. This strategy worked well for me. It works well for global corporations, too. Consider an example from McDonald's.

McDonald's is a prime example of how marketing can transform public perception. Few people would argue that McDonald's makes the best cheeseburger they've ever tasted. Yet statistics show that McDonald's sells more cheeseburgers than any other restaurant.

Why?

McDonald's strategic marketing efforts, brand consistency, and relentless focus on success bring results that shareholders want. Shareholders want the restaurant to be profitable. They created a marketing strategy, and they executed their plan. They've built a tribe of followers that recognizes the golden arches—a tactic.

We can learn a lot from that example.

Building a Positive Narrative

To prepare for success after prison, we need effective strategies. Those strategies should include tactics to help others see our commitment to reconciliation.

Step 1: We should build a record of incremental progress that supports our commitment to success.

Step 2: We should memorialize how we've worked to prepare.

Step 3: We should show how we've contributed to the making of a better culture or community, documenting the story of how many people we've helped.

Those micro steps, over time, can help us restore confidence and help others begin to view us from a different lens. Instead of judging us for the decisions that led to our criminal conviction, they begin to see us for how we responded. This effort helps us build trust, and we can translate our body of work into a better reputation.

No one will know what we've done if we do not document our preparations for success upon release. Without a personal action plan, we can get stuck with a bad reputation, limiting our opportunities.

When I visit prisons to present the importance of preparing for success upon release, many people tell me how hard they work. I engage members of the audience with a question about reading.

Could you tell me how many books you've read since you began serving your sentence?

Typically, people say that they read a lot.

But saying "I read a lot of books" is not nearly as powerful as giving data:

"I've read 92 books and I've written 92 book reports. Each report shows the reason I chose to read the book, what I learned, and why reading it will contribute to my success upon release."

If a person can show all 92 reports in a central location, he has an asset—a resource. He can use that resource to validate his self-directed effort to prepare for success. People will begin to view him from a different lens. He isn't the kind of person who talks about wanting to succeed upon release. Instead, he is the kind of person who knows how to prepare for success.

The harder a person works to memorialize his preparations for success, the more credibility and trust he builds. Those records become transformational, improving an online reputation. It's part of a personal marketing strategy, empowering people to communicate with a broader audience.

We should work to build a tribe of advocates.

Building a Tribe: Helping Others Succeed

Many people in prison use their time to help others. They should record the efforts they're making to build better communities. For example, if a person led a class that resulted in five people earning their GED, then it would be helpful for the person to document those efforts. We want people to work toward becoming good citizens, and we want them to show the impact they're having on building safer communities.

This strategy will help others see them differently.

To assist community members, we're investing in building data graphs. If a person influences five people to prepare for success, and those five people go on to influence five more people, a person's influence grows in geometric proportions. Recording those contributions will help a person tell a more compelling story about working to reconcile with society.

We want people to be extraordinary and compelling. For that reason, we encourage participants to help others commit to this strategy of preparing for success upon release. To the extent we're able, our nonprofit will continue producing resources to help.

Just as McDonald's built its empire through strategic marketing and consistent messaging, we can redefine our image by showcasing positive contributions, transparency, a commitment to personal growth, and pursuing excellence.

Start building a tribe. Show your positive influences on improving your community, and use that story to open new opportunities. Personal marketing is not about erasing one's history but embracing growth, redemption, and a determination to be a law-abiding, contributing citizen.

Made in the USA
Monee, IL
19 October 2024

67827133R00050